Ship or Sheep?

An intermediate pronunciation course

Ann Baker

with cartoons by Leslie Marshall

D0755786

CAMBRIDGE
UNIVERSITY PRESS

PUBLISHED BY THE PRESS SYNDICATE OF THE UNIVERSITY OF CAMBRIDGE
The Pitt Building, Trumpington Street, Cambridge, United Kingdom

CAMBRIDGE UNIVERSITY PRESS
The Edinburgh Building, Cambridge CB2 2RU, UK
40 West 20th Street, New York, NY 10011–4211, USA
477 Williamstown Road, Port Melbourne, VIC 3207, Australia
Ruiz de Alarcón 13, 28014 Madrid, Spain
Dock House, The Waterfront, Cape Town 8001, South Africa

http://www.cambridge.org

First published 1977
Second edition 1981
Twenty-seventh printing 2003

Printed in the United Kingdom at the University Press, Cambridge

A catalogue record for this book is available from the British Library

ISBN 0 521 28354 X Ship or Sheep? Student's Book
ISBN 0 521 26358 1 Ship or Sheep? Set of 3 cassettes
ISBN 0 521 28580 1 Introducing English Pronunciation Teacher's Book

Contents

To the student

This book has been written to help you recognise and pronounce English sounds. To make it interesting and fun to learn, there are lots of different types of exercise. When you do them by yourself or in class, you will realise that you are not only learning how to produce sounds: you are also practising the skills needed to communicate in real life.

The sounds are separated into two different sections but you do not have to work your way through the book from left to right. You can choose the units which practise sounds you find especially difficult, or study vowels and consonants together.

All exercises with this symbol ▭ are recorded on cassette. The key symbol ⚷ tells you that the complete sentences for the tests are given at the back of the book. Answers to the recorded listening exercises in the Review units are also given.

To the teacher

This book is designed to train students to recognise and produce English sounds. The basic premise behind it is that pronunciation material should be meaningful and easily understood.

The material has been developed for use in the classroom as well as for students working alone. Cassettes accompany the book and a Teacher's Book (forthcoming) will provide extra guidance and help for teachers.

Each of the forty-nine units in this book practises a different sound and provides a variety of activities for this purpose. Stress and intonation, as well as sounds, are important for successful communication in English and aspects of these are also introduced and practised.

Students may wish to work their way through the book using lessons from Sections A (vowels) and B (consonants) simultaneously. Or they may prefer to choose units which are helpful for their own particular problems.

The symbol ▭ indicates exercises which have been recorded on the cassettes. The key symbol ⚿ following the tests indicates that the text is given at the back of the book. Answers to the recorded listening exercises in the Review Units are also given.

Section A

Vocabulary

First learn the words you will need to study how to make the sounds in this section.

Your mouth

1 This is your mouth.

2 Open your mouth

3 Close your mouth.

4 Open your mouth a little.

5 Open your mouth a little more.

Vocabulary

Your tongue

tongue

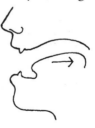

the front of your tongue

the back of your tongue

Moving your tongue

Put your tongue forward.

Put your tongue back.

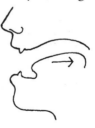

Put your tongue up.

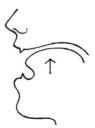

Put your tongue down.

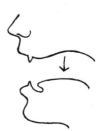

Put your tongue forward and up.

Put your tongue down and back.

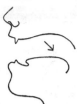

Practise i:
eat, easy, he, we, she

Practise ɑ:
ask, answer, arm, car

Unit 1 i: sheep

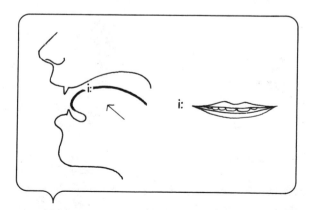

Open your mouth very little to make the sound i:.
i: is a long sound.

3

Practice 1 Listen and repeat:

bean   heel   meal

peel   sheep

cheap

seat

eat   leek   cheeks

Practice 2 Listen and repeat:

Edith	see	eating
evening	tea	Peter
easy	pea	meat
Jean	three	
cheese		

4

Dialogue   ## In a restaurant

Peter: *What would you like to eat, Edith?*
Edith: *A meat sandwich.*
Peter: *Jean? Would you like a meat sandwich or a cheese sandwich?*
Jean: *A cheese sandwich, please, Peter.*
Waiter: *Good evening.*
Peter: *Good evening. We'll have one meat sandwich and two cheese sandwiches.*
Edith: *And three teas, please!*
Waiter: (writing down the order) *One meat sandwich . . . two cheese sandwiches . . . and . . . three teas.*

Intonation   ### Questions with 'or'

These have a falling tune at the end.
The parts of words which are in
blacker type are louder, or stressed.

Would you like **cóff**ee or **têa**?
Would you like **vêal** or **bêef**?

Would you like **cóff**ee or **mîlk** or
têa?

Now practise with somebody,
using this menu.

Example

Would you like leek soup or pea
soup?
Leek soup, please.

MENU

Soup:
leek soup OR pea soup

Meat:
Veal OR beef

Vegetables:
beans OR peas

Sweets:
cheesecake OR ice-cream
OR peaches

coffee OR tea

Conversation Using the menu, practise in a group of four people:

You are in a restaurant.
One person is the waiter.
One person asks the questions: Would you like . . . or . . .?
Then you must give your order to the waiter.
The waiter must remember the order.

Unit 2 ɪ ship

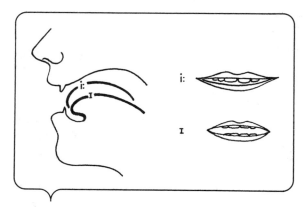

First practise the sound i: (see page 3).
Then open your mouth a *little* more.
i: is a long sound.
ɪ is a short sound.

Practice 1 Listen and repeat:

sound 1 sound 2

sheep ship

bean bin

eat it

seat sit

leek lick

cheeks chicks

Test

Tick the words you recognise in the sentences you hear:

ɪ a) sheep; b) ship
2 a) bean; b) bin
3 a) cheeks; b) chicks
4 a) cheap; b) chip
5 a) heel; b) hill
6 a) peel; b) pill

Practice 2

Listen and repeat:

it's	Tim	fifty
isn't	film	sixty
ill	minutes	
Indians	beginning	
interesting	Mrs Smith	

Dialogue

An interesting film

Bill:	*Is Tim in?*
Lyn:	*Is he coming to the pictures?*
Mrs Smith:	*Tim's ill.*
Bill:	*Here he is! Hello, Tim.*
Tim:	*Hello, Bill.*
Lyn:	*Are you ill, Tim?*
Tim:	*Is it an interesting film?*
Lyn:	*It's 'Big Jim and the Indians'.*
Bill:	*And it begins in six minutes.*
Mrs Smith:	*If you're ill, Tim ...*
Tim:	*Quick! Or we'll miss the beginning of the film!*

Stress

Numbers

Listen and repeat:

three	thir**teen**	**thir**ty	3	ɪ3	30
four	four**teen**	**for**ty	4	ɪ4	40
five	fif**teen**	**fif**ty	5	ɪ5	50
six	six**teen**	**six**ty	6	ɪ6	60
seven	seven**teen**	**sev**enty	7	ɪ7	70

8

Unit 3   e (pen)

| **eight** | eigh**teen** | **eigh**ty | 8 | 18 | 80 |
| **nine** | nine**teen** | **nine**ty | 9 | 19 | 90 |

Game   Mini bingo

Play in a group of five people.
One person calls out the numbers above in any order.
The others each choose one of the boxes A, B, C or D below.
Cross out each number in your box as it is called (or put a
small piece of paper on top of each number as it is called).
The first person to cross out all his numbers wins.

A

13	3	80
7	19	50
17	90	8

B

60	4	16
20	30	13
70	5	90

C

5	15	16
70	90	3
40	7	18

D

60	6	15
8	14	17
9	90	80

Unit 3   e   pen

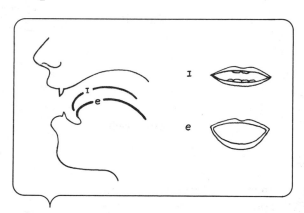

First practise the sound ı (see page 6).
Then open your mouth a *little* more.
e is a short sound.

Practice 1   Listen and repeat:

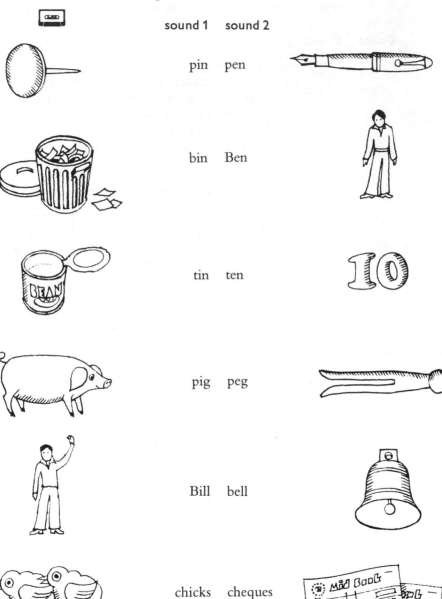

	sound 1	sound 2	
	pin	pen	
	bin	Ben	
	tin	ten	
	pig	peg	
	Bill	bell	
	chicks	cheques	

Unit 3   e (pen)

Test

Tick the words you recognise in the sentences you hear:
1 a) pin; b) pen
2 a) pig; b) peg
3 a) tins; b) tens
4 a) sit; b) set
5 a) Jinny; b) Jenny
6 a) picked; b) pecked

Practice 2

Listen and repeat:

any	spend	Jenny
everybody	friend	jealous
everything	left	America
Eddie	shelf	expensive cigarettes
Ellen	ten pence	help yourself

Dialogue

An expensive holiday

Eddie: *Hello, Ellen! Hello, Ben! Hello, Jenny!*
Ben: *Hello, Eddie. Have a cigarette.*
Eddie: *Thanks, Ben.*
Ellen: *Help yourself to whisky.*
Jenny: *It's on the shelf.*
Ben: *How did you spend your holiday, Eddie?*
Eddie: *I went to America with a friend.*
Everybody: *Well!*
Ellen: *We're all jealous.*
Ben: *Was it expensive?*
Eddie: *Yes. Very. I've spent everything.*
Jenny: *Haven't you any money left?*
Eddie: *Yes, Jenny. Ten pence!*

Intonation

Statements usually have a falling tune at the end.
'Wh' questions (Who? What? Why? When? Where? How?)
usually have a falling tune at the end.
Yes/No questions usually have a rising tune at the end.

Examples:

'Wh' question: How did you spend your **hol**iday?

Statement: I went to Amĕrica.

Yes/No question: Was it expensive?

Statement: **Yes. Very.**

Conversation   Practise this dialogue.
Use the place names below.

Kent   **Venice**   **Belgium**   **Denmark**   **Edinburgh**

How did you spend your holiday?
I went to ...
Was it expensive?
Yes. Very.

Unit 4   æ man

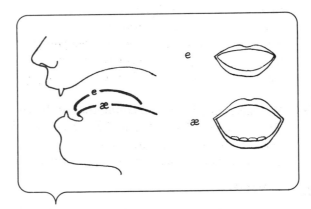

First practise the sound **e** (see page 9).
Then open your mouth a *little* more.

Practice 1   Listen and repeat:

| | **sound 1** | **sound 2** |

x   axe

pen   pan

men   man

said   sad

beg   bag

bread   Brad

13

Test

Tick the words you recognise in the sentences you hear:
1 a) pen; b) pan
2 a) men; b) man
3 a) said; b) sad
4 a) gem; b) jam
5 a) pet; b) pat
6 a) bed; b) bad

Practice 2

Listen and repeat:

apple	Anne	camera
perhaps	Amsterdam	lavatory
passenger	Alice	travelling
hijacker	Miss Allen	handbag
jacket		left hand
black slacks		Miss Bradley

Diaglogue

A bad hijacker

Hostess Bradley: *Alice! Perhaps that passenger is a hijacker!*

Hostess Allen: *Which passenger, Anne? That sad man with the camera? He's wearing black slacks and a jacket.*

Hostess Bradley: *No. That fat lady with the big black handbag in her left hand.*

Hostess Allen: *Is she standing next to the lavatory?*

Hostess Bradley: *Yes. She's travelling to Amsterdam.*

Hostess Allen: *You're mad, Anne, I don't understand.*

Hostess Bradley: *You see, when she went into the lavatory she didn't have that handbag in her hand, and now she's . . .*

Fat lady: (clapping her hands) EVERYBODY STAND! *I'm a hijacker. And in this handbag I have a . . .*

Handbag: BANG!

Unit 4   æ (man)

Stress   In English some words are stressed at the end: per**haps**

be**low**

a**bout**

Some words are stressed in the middle: be**ginn**ing

conver**sat**ion

But most words are stressed at the beginning:

camera	**hand**bag	**pic**tures	**crick**et bat
family	**sand**wich	**wait**ing	**aer**oplane
apple	**prac**tise	**air**port	**hi**jacker
jacket	**pass**enger	**wo**man	

Conversation   Practise this conversation about the passengers in the picture
below. They are in the airport waiting to get on the aeroplane.

Example:

Student A: Perhaps that passenger is a hijacker.
Student B: Do you mean the man with the **black slacks**?
Student A: No. The woman with the **black hand**bag.

red hat

black
slacks

cat

cricket bat

black handbag

15

jacket

family

sandwich

apple

camera

Unit 5 ∧ cup

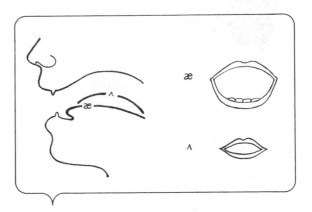

First practise the sound æ (see page 12).
Then put your tongue back a little.
∧ is a very short sound.

Practice 1 Listen and repeat:

	sound 1	sound 2	
	cap	cup	
	hat	hut	
	sack	suck	
	ban	bun	
	bag	bug	
	hag	hug	

Unit 5   ʌ (cup)

Test   Tick the words you recognise in the sentences you hear:

1 a) cap; b) cup   4 a) mad; b) mud
2 a) hat; b) hut   5 a) hang; b) hung
3 a) bag; b) bug   6 a) ran; b) run

Practice 2   Listen and repeat:

ugly   must   love
untrue   much   lovely
unhappy   lunch   honey
understand Sunny   worry
shut up   cousin   company
just once   Russ   wonderful

Dialogue   # I love you

Russ: *Honey, why are you so sad?*
        (Janet says nothing)
Russ: *Honey, why are you so unhappy? I don't understand.*
Janet: *You don't love me, Russ!*
Russ: *But, honey, I love you very much.*
Janet: *That's untrue. You love my cousin, Sunny. You think she's lovely and I'm ugly.*
Russ: *Janet, just once last month I took Sunny out for lunch. You mustn't worry. I like your company much better than Sunny's.*
Janet: *Oh, shut up, Russ.*
Russ: *But, honey, I think you're wonderful. You mustn't...*
Janet: *Oh,* SHUT UP!

Intonation   Making a list

Listen and repeat:

He bought a cup and some nuts.

He bought a cup, some nuts and some honey.

He bought a cup, some nuts, some honey, and a brush.

Game   'My uncle went to London'

Practise this game first with the class, then in groups of five or six people. Choose any words from the list below.

Example:

Student A : *My uncle went to London and he spent a lot of money.*
             He bought a bus.
Student B : *My uncle went to London and he spent a lot of money.*
             He bought a bus and a dozen buns.

Each student adds something to the list, and you must
remember what the other students have said.

Practise saying the words before you start:

a cup	some butter
a cupboard	some honey
a bus	one onion
a bottle of rum	a brush
a hundred buttons	a rubber duck
some nuts	a dozen buns
a tongue	an ugly monkey
a blood sausage	a lovely butterfly
some comfortable gloves	some coloured sunglasses

Unit 6 ɑː   heart

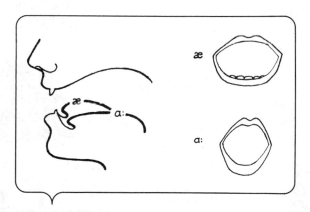

Put your tongue down and back.
ɑː is a long sound.

Practice 1   Listen and repeat:

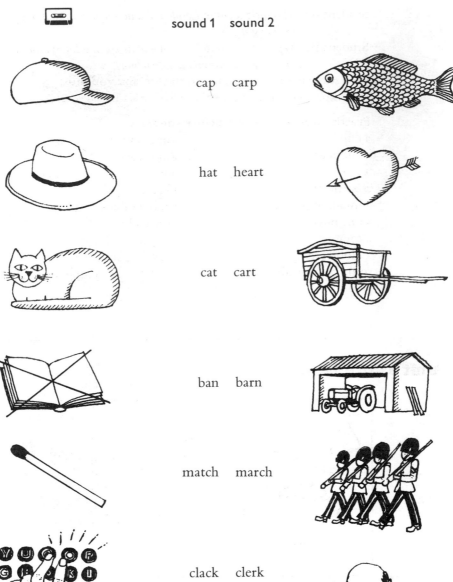

	sound 1	sound 2
	cap	carp
	hat	heart
	cat	cart
	ban	barn
	match	march
	clack	clerk

Practice 2 Listen and repeat:

	sound 1	sound 2

cup   carp

hut   heart

cut   cart

bun   barn

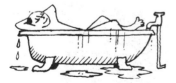 

much   march

cluck   clerk

Unit 6   ɑː (heart)

Test

Tick the words you recognise in the sentences you hear:

1 a) hat; b) hut; c) heart   4 a) bun; b) barn
2 a) cat; b) cut; c) cart   5 a) come; b) calm
3 a) cap; b) cup; c) carp   6 a) Patty's; b) parties

Practice 3

Listen and repeat:

Ah!	marvellous	guitar	smart
Arnold	bar	Barbara	Martin
So they are!	far	Margaret	Martha
can't	car	Charles	dark
garden	star		laugh
			photograph

Dialogue

At a party

Margaret: *Where's your glass, Barbara?*
Barbara: *It's on the bar.*
Martin: *Barbara! Margaret! Come into the garden!*
           Martha and Charles are dancing in the dark.
Margaret: *In the garden? What a laugh!*
Barbara: *So they are! They're dancing on the grass!*
Margaret: *They're dancing under the stars!*
Martin: *And Arnold's playing his guitar.*
Barbara: *Doesn't Martha look smart!*
Margaret: *Look at Charles! What a marvellous dancer!*
Barbara: *Ah! Let's take a photograph of Martha and Charles.*
Martin: *We can't. It's too dark.*

Intonation

Listen and repeat:

What a **fast car**!

What a **funny dan**cer!

What a **mar**vellous **pho**tograph!

What a fan**tastic** gui**tar**!

Conversation

Practise this conversation about the pictures below:
A: Look at that car!
B: What a fast car!

| **dark** | **dir**ty |
| **fast** | **mar**vellous |

22

smart un**usual**
funny fan**tas**tic

glass **car**pet gui**tar**

dancer

car

star

photograph **scarf**

Unit 7 Review

1	2	3	4	5	6
iː	ɪ	e	æ	ʌ	ɑː
bean	bin	Ben	ban	bun	barn
beat	bit	bet	bat	but	Bart
bead	bid	bed	bad	bud	bard
peak	pick	peck	pack	Puck	park

Listening practice

When you hear one of these words or sounds, say which number it is.

Examples:

ɑː   bid
Students: sound 6   Students: sound 2

23

Now listen and repeat:

eat	eggs	mat	sit	cups	grass
seat	any	ham	fish	buns	garden
tea	ready	apple	chips	lunch	tart

Reading   Lunch on the grass

Ben: *Is lunch ready?*
Anne: *Yes. Let's eat lunch in the garden.*
Ben: *Shall we sit on this seat?*
Anne: *Let's sit on this mat on the grass.*
Ben: *Is it fish and chips for lunch?*
Anne: *No. It's ham and eggs.*
Ben: *Have you any buns and ham?*
Anne: *Yes. And cups of tea and apple tart.*

Unit 8   ɒ   clock

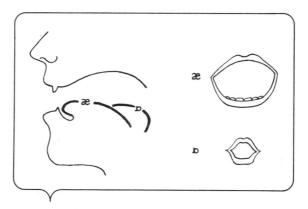

First practise the sound æ (see page 12).
Then put your tongue slightly back and bring your lips
slightly forward.
ɒ is a short sound.

24

Practice 1   Listen and repeat:

	sound 1	sound 2	
	hat	hot	
	cat	cot	
	Pat	pot	
	sack	sock	
	tap	top	
	backs	box	

Test

Tick the words you recognise in the sentences you hear:

1 a) cat; b) cot
2 a) sack; b) sock
3 a) tap; b) top
4 a) Tammy; b) Tommy
5 a) baddie; b) body
6 a) black; b) block

Practice 2

Listen and repeat:

off	got	sorry
often	bottle	holiday
on	want	horrible
'Onwash'	what's wrong	washing
a long job	Mrs Bloggs	popular

Dialogue

TV advertisement for 'Onwash'

Voice A: *What's wrong with you, Mrs Bloggs?*
Mrs Bloggs: *What's wrong with me? I want a holiday from this*
              horrible job of washing socks!
Voice B: *Buy a bottle of 'Onwash', Mrs Bloggs!*
Voice C: *'Onwash' is so soft and strong.*
Voice D: *You don't want lots of hot water with 'Onwash'.*
Voice A: *It's not a long job with 'Onwash'.*
Voice B: *Use 'Onwash' often.*
Voice C: *You won't be sorry when you've got 'Onwash'.*
Voice D: *Everybody wants 'Onwash'.*
Everybody: *'Onwash' is so popular!*

Intonation

A suggestion sounds polite
and friendly:

Have a **hol**iday, Mrs Bloggs.

A command sounds less
friendly:

Have a **hol**iday, Mrs Bloggs.

Stop **wash**ing, Mrs Bloggs.   Stop **wash**ing, Mrs Bloggs.

Don't drop that **pot**, Mrs   Don't drop that **pot**, Mrs
Bloggs.   Bloggs.

Put it on the **box**, Mrs Bloggs.   Put it on the **box**, Mrs Bloggs.

Competition   Friendly or unfriendly?

Divide the class into two teams.
The teacher reads the following sentences.
Students take turns to decide if he's friendly or unfriendly.
Score a point for each correct answer.

Put these socks in the **box**.   Don't wash these **socks**.
Put it on top of the **clock**.   Don't borrow Tom's **watch**.
Make the coffee **hot**.   Don't go to the wrong **off**ice.
Go to the **hos**pital.   Don't go to the wrong **res**taurant.
See a **doc**tor.   Buy some bi**noc**ulars.

Unit 9   ɔ: ball

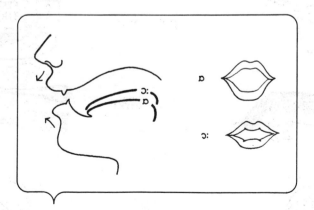

First practise the sound ɒ (see page 24).
Then put the back of your tongue up a *little*.
ɔ: is a long sound.

Practice 1 Listen and repeat:

| | sound 1 | sound 2 | |

 Don Dawn

 cod cord

 cot caught

pot port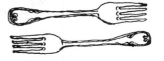

fox forks

 spots sports

Unit 9 ɔː (ball)

Tick the words you recognise in the sentences you hear:

1 a) spots; b) sports
2 a) pots; b) ports
3 a) cod; b) cord
4 a) shot; b) short
5 a) Rod; b) roared
6 a) what a; b) water 🔑

Practice 2

Listen and repeat:

or	Paul	awful
score	towards	airport
four	audience	reporter
all	forward	forty
always	George	walking
footballer	'the Roarers'	York

A football match

the score board → / the goal keeper ↓ / the ball ↓

SCORE
Roarers 4
York 44

→ a fallen footballer

a forward ←

Dialogue

Sports report from Channel 4

Announcer: *This morning the Roarers football team arrived back from York. Paul Short is our sports reporter, and he was at the airport.*

Paul Short: *Good morning. This is Paul Short. All the footballers are walking towards me. Here's George Ball, the goalkeeper. Good morning, George.*

29

Unit 9   ɔː (ball)

George Ball:	*Good morning. Are you a reporter?*
Paul Short:	*Yes. I'm from Channel 4. Please tell our audience about the football match with York.*
George Ball:	*Well, it was awful. We lost. And the score was four, forty-four. But it wasn't my fault.*
Paul Short:	*Whose fault was it?*
George Ball:	*The forwards.*
Paul Short:	*The forwards?*
George Ball:	*Yes. The forwards. They were always falling down or losing the ball!*

Intonation   Surprise

A: Mr Short always plays football in the morning.

B: In the **morn**ing?

C: Mr **Short**?

D: **Foot**ball?

E: **Al**ways?

In this conversation B, C, D and E are all surprised by what A says. B is surprised that he plays *in the morning*. C is surprised that *Mr Short* plays. D is surprised that he plays *football*. E is surprised that he *always* plays.

Practise in pairs. B must sound surprised about the part of the sentence in italics.

Example:

I saw Audrey *at the airport*.

A: I saw Audrey at the **air**port.

B: At the **air**port?

A: *Yes.* At the **air**port.

1 I've put the ball *in the drawer*.
2 *It's too warm* to go walking.
3 Dawn wrote a report *in shorthand*.
4 George has bought *forty-five forks*.

30

5 I'm going to buy *a horse.*
6 You ought to get up *at four in the morning.*
7 I saw *George* when I was *in New York.*
8 It's *your fault.*

Unit 10 ʊ book

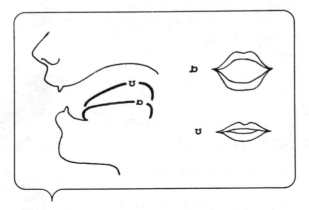

First practise the sound ɒ (see page 24).
Then put the back of your tongue forward and up a little.
ʊ is a short sound.

Practice 1   Listen and repeat:

sound 1   sound 2

pot   put

cock   cook

god   good

lock   look

rock   rook

box   books

32

Test   Tick the words you recognise in the sentences you hear:

1 a) cock; b) cook
2 a) lock; b) look
3 a) god; b) good
4 a) cod; b) could
5 a) Poss; b) Puss
6 a) Brockhurst; b) Brookhurst

Practice 2   Listen and repeat:

put	full	cookery books
look	woman	shouldn't you
good	bedroom	didn't you
foot	living-room	Mr Cook
could	bookshelf	

Dialogue   # A lost book

Mr Cook :   *Woman! Could you tell me where you've put my book?*

Mrs Cook : *Isn't it on the bookshelf?*

Mr Cook :   *No. The bookshelf is full of your cookery books.*

Mrs Cook : *Then you should look in the bedroom, shouldn't you?*

Mr Cook :   *I've looked. You took that book and put it somewhere, didn't you?*

Mrs Cook : *The living-room?*

Mr Cook :   *No. I've looked. I'm going to put all my books in a box and lock it!*

Mrs Cook : *Look, Mr Cook! It's on the floor next to your foot.*

Mr Cook :   *Ah! Good!*

Intonation   Question tags

Listen and repeat:

should you?   **could** you?   **would** he?

She couldn't **cook**,   **could** she?

He wouldn't **look**,   **would** he?

33

Practise in pairs:

Example: She couldn't cook.

A: She couldn't co͡ok, co͡uld she?

B: No, she co͡uldn't.

1 He couldn't play **foot**ball.
2 You couldn't cook a cake without **sug**ar.
3 You wouldn't like to meet a **bull**.
4 You wouldn't like to meet a **wolf**.
5 He shouldn't put good books on the **cook**er.
6 He shouldn't look at that **wom**an.
7 You couldn't cook a **book**.
8 They shouldn't read these **books**.

Unit 11   u: boot

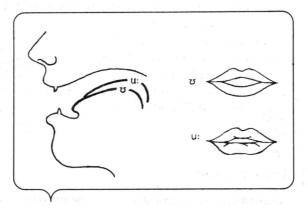

First practise the sound ʊ again (see page 31).
ʊ is a short sound.
Then put your tongue up and back.
u: is a long sound.

Practice 1 Listen and repeat:

sound 1   sound 2

        look   Luke

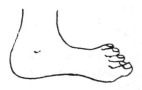   pull   pool

   full   fool

   foot   boot

Test Tick the words you recognise in the sentences you hear:

1 a) look; b) Luke
2 a) full; b) fool
3 a) pull; b) pool
4 a) fullish; b) foolish

35

Practice 2   Listen and repeat:

Sue	June	soup
Prue	unit	stupid
shoe	afternoon	nuisance
threw	excuse me	Miss Luke
twenty-two	chewing gum	
It was YOU!	rude	

Dialogue   # In a good school

Miss Luke: *Good afternoon, girls.*
Girls: *Good afternoon, Miss Luke.*
Miss Luke: *This afternoon we're going to learn how to cook soup.*
Open your books at unit twenty-two.
Prue: *Excuse me, Miss Luke.*
Miss Luke: *Yes, Prue?*
Prue: *There's some chewing gum on your shoe.*
Miss Luke: *Who threw their chewing gum on the floor? Was it*
you, Prue?
Prue: *No, Miss Luke. It was June.*
Miss Luke: *Who?*
Prue: *June Cook.*
June: *It wasn't me, stupid. It was Sue.*
Sue: *It was you!*
June: *It wasn't me, you stupid fool. My mouth's full of*
chewing gum. Look, Miss Luke!
Sue: *Stop pulling my hair, June. It was you!*
June: *YOU!*
Sue: *YOU!*
Miss Luke: *Excuse me! You're being very rude. You two nuisances*
can stay in school this afternoon instead of going to the
swimming pool.

Stress   Read this conversation. Make the stressed words louder.

A: Ex**cuse me**.
B: **Yes**?
A: **Could** you **tell** me **where** I can **get** some **good shoe**laces?
B: **Yes**. There's a **shop next** to the **su**permarket that **sells**
very **good shoe**laces. **I'm go**ing **there too**.

36

Conversation   Practise in pairs. Use the words below.

Excuse me.
Yes?
Could you tell me where I can get some good ¹ . . . . ?
Yes. There's a shop next to the ² . . . . that sells very
good ¹ . . . . I'm going there too.

Practise these words first:

¹**shoe**laces	²**su**permarket
toothpaste	**swimm**ing pool
football boots	**fruit** shop
chewing gum	**tool** shop
fruit juice	**wool** shop
cookery books	**news**paper stand

Unit 12   ɜː   girl

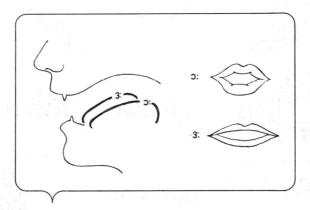

First practise the sound ɔː (see page 27).
Then put your tongue forward and up a little.
ɜː is a long sound.

Practice 1   Listen and repeat:

	sound 1	sound 2	
	four	fur	
	torn	turn	
	Paul	Pearl	
	warm	worm	
	'ward	word	*Two words*
	walker	worker	

38

Practice 2 Listen and repeat:

	sound 1	sound 2	
	ten	turn	
	Ben	burn	
	bed	bird	
	head	heard	
	west	worst	
	kennel	colonel	

Practice 3   Listen and repeat:

        sound 1   sound 2

        shut   shirt

        huts   hurts

        bun   burn

        bud   bird

        bug   berg

        gull   girl

Test   Tick the words you recognise in the sentences you hear:
1 a) bed; b) bud; c) bird
2 a) Ben's; b) buns; c) burns
3 a) ward; b) word
4 a) walk; b) work
5 a) short; b) shirt
6 a) or; b) er

Practice 4   Listen and repeat:

er	Herbert		
sir	Sherman	worst	skirts
carly	Turner	thirsty	shirts
world	weren't	dirty	nurse
Thursday	colonel	Burton	Curse these nurses!

Dialogue   # The worst nurse

Sir Herbert: *Nurse!*
Colonel Burton: *Nurse! I'm thirsty!*
Sir Herbert: *Nurse! My head hurts!*
Colonel Burton: NURSE!
Sir Herbert: *Curse these nurses!*
Colonel Burton: *Nurse Sherman always wears such dirty shirts.*
Sir Herbert: *And such short skirts.*
Colonel Burton: *She never arrives at work early.*
Sir Herbert: *She and ... er ... Nurse Turner weren't at work on Thursday, were they?*
Colonel Burton: *No, they weren't.*
Sir Herbert: *Nurse Sherman is the worst nurse in the ward, isn't she?*
Colonel Burton: *No, she isn't. She's the worst nurse in the world!*

Intonation   Listen and repeat:

we͡re we?
we͡re you?
we͡re they?
We weren't e͡arly, we͡re we?

41

Practise in pairs.

Example: We weren't early.
A: We weren't early, were we?
B: No, we weren't.

Example: You weren't early.
A: You weren't early, were you?
B: No, I wasn't.

1 We weren't the worst.
2 You weren't first.
3 These girls weren't German.
4 The curtains weren't dirty.
5 We weren't learning Turkish.
6 These birds weren't hers.
7 These girls weren't walking to work.
8 You weren't thirsty.

Unit 13 ə a camera

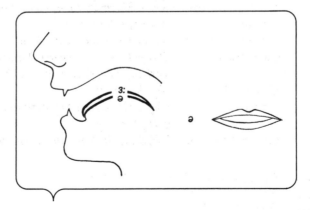

First make the sound ɜː (see page 37).
This is a long sound.
Then make it very short. This is ə.
ə is a very short sound.

Unit 13   ə (a camera)

Practice 1   We use the sound ə in words and syllables that are not
 important. Practise these. In the words on the right the spelling
has been changed to show you when to make the sound ə.

(i) Listen and repeat each one twice:

a photograph of   1   ə photəgraph əf Barbərə
Barbara

a glass of water   2   ə glass əf watə

a pair of binoculars 3   ə pair əf binoculəs

a photograph   4
of her mother   ə photəgraph
and father   əf hə mothər ənd fathə

a book about   5   ə book əbout
South America   South əmericə

(ii) Now cover the words on the left above and practise
questions and answers.

Example:

What's in picture two?
ə glass əf watə

43

Unit 13   ə (a camera)

(iii) Listen and repeat:

| Look at the clock. | Look ət thə clock. |
| What's the time? | What's thə time? |

It's six o'clock. It's six ə'clock.

It's a quarter to seven. It's ə quartə tə sevən.

(iv) Now practise these

Example:

A: What's thə time?
B: It's ə quartə tə twelve.

Practice 2

Read this story aloud. The spelling has been changed to show you when to make the sound ə.

Barbərə spent Satəday aftənoon looking ət ə beautifəl book əbout South əmericə.

'I want tə go tə South əmericə,' she said tə həself.

Thə next morning, when Barbərə woke up it wəs six ə'clock, ənd hə brothəs ənd sistəs wə still əsleep. Barbərə looked ət thəm, ənd closed hər eyes əgain.

Then she quiətly got out əf bed ənd started tə pack hə suitcase.

She took səme comfətəble clothes out əf thə cupbəd. She packed ə pair əf binoculəs ənd hə sistə's camərə. She packed ə photəgraph əf həself ənd one əf hə mothər ənd fathə.

'I mustn't fəget tə have səme breakfəst, she said tə həself. Bət then she looked ət thə clock. It wəs ə quartə tə seven.

'I'll jəst drink ə glass əf watə,' she said.

'ə glass əf watə,' she said.

'Watə,' she said, ənd opened hər eyes.

44

She wəs still in hə bed, ənd hə brothəs ənd sistəs wə laughing ət hə.

'Tell əs what you wə dreaming əbout,' they said tə hə.

Bət Barbərə didn't answə. She wəs thinking about hə wondəful journey tə South əmericə.

Practice 3   Weak forms

Wəs she dreaming?   Yes, she **was**.

This is the sound ə.   This is the strong form of 'was'
This is the weak form of 'was'.   This is a different sound.

Listen and repeat:

Wəs she thinking about South America?   Yes, she **was**.
Wə her brothers and sisters asleep?   Yes, they **were**.
Də they like reading?   Yes, they **do**.
Həve you read about South America?   Yes, I **have**.
Dəs your friend like reading?   Yes, he **does**.
əm I talking to myself?   Yes, I **am**.
ə we working hard?   Yes, we **are**.
Həs your friend been to South America?   Yes, he **has**.
Cən you swim?   Yes, I **can**.

Test   Tick the words you recognise in the sentences you hear:

1 a) **has**; b) həs
2 a) **can**; b) cən
3 a) **was**; b) wəs
4 a) **does**; b) dəs
5 a) **am**; b) əm
6 a) **them**; b) thəm

Dialogue   Shopping

The words in italics are weak forms and have the sound ə here.

A: I'm going *to the* | post office.
                      | library.

B: *Can* you buy something for me *at the* | supermarket?
                                            | tobacconist's?

A: *But the* | supermarket | is *a* | long way | *from the* | post office.
             | tobacconist's | | mile | | library.

45

B: No. Not that | supermarket. | Not *the* one *that's* next *to the*
tobacconist's. |

| cinema. | I mean *the* one *that's* near *the* | fruit shop.
| swimming pool. | | butcher's.

A: Oh, yes. Well, what do you want?

B: *Some* | cigarettes *and a* | box *of* matches | *and an* | envelope.
| cigars | tin *of* sweets | | address book.

Unit 14   Review

1	2	3	4	5
ɒ	ɔ:	ʊ	u:	ɜ:
Polly	Paul	pull	pool	Pearl
folly	fall	full	fool	furl
cod	cord	could	cooed	curd
what	ward	would	wooed	word

Listening practice   When you hear one of these words or sounds, say which number it is.

Examples:
ɒ   Pearl
Students: sound 1   Students: sound 5

Now look at the words below:
The words on the left have the sound ə here. Listen and repeat:

at	look ət it
of	full əf it
to them	talk tə thəm
the	thə pool
a	ə cord
an or	ən hour ə two
was	it wəs too long
and	Polly ənd Paul

46

Reading   Polly and Paul

John : *Did you fall into the pool, Pearl?*

Pearl : *No. Polly and Paul pushed me into the pool, and that pool is full of dirty water.*

John : *What did you do?*

Pearl : *I felt really foolish because my skirt was too long and I saw Mr Lukey looking at me.*

John : *What did Mr Lukey do?*

Pearl : *Mr Lukey was very good. First he got a cord and threw it to me. Then he pulled me out of the pool.*

John : *Hm. Polly and Paul. I'll talk to these two. They're the worst children in the world. Perhaps I'll lock them in their rooms for an hour or two.*

Unit 15 eɪ   tail

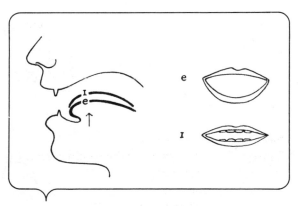

This has two sounds : e and ɪ (see pages 9 and 6).
First make the sound e.
Now make it longer : eee.
Then add ɪ. This is very short.
eeeɪ.

47

Unit 15 eɪ (tail)

Practice 1 Listen and repeat:

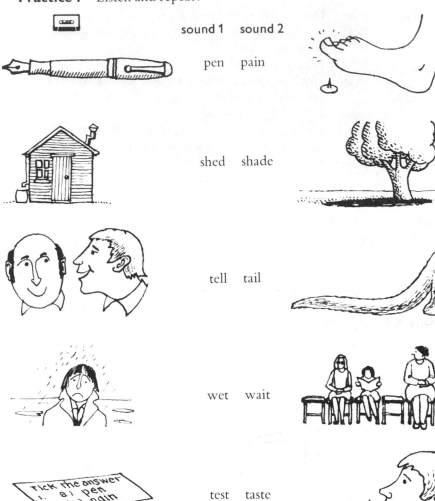

	sound 1	sound 2	
	pen	pain	
	shed	shade	
	tell	tail	
	wet	wait	
	test	taste	
	pepper	paper	

Test

Tick the words you recognise in the sentences you hear:

1 a) pen; b) pain   4 a) let; b) late
2 a) shed; b) shade   5 a) letter; b) later
3 a) pepper; b) paper 6 a) get; b) gate

Practice 2

Listen and repeat:

Hey!	made	late
say	afraid	waiting
Mr Grey	train	eight-eight
may	timetable	station
they	ages	Baker Street
today	changed	April
railway		

Dialogue

At the railway station

(Mr Grey is waiting at the railway station for a train.)
Mr Grey: *Hey! This train's late! I've been waiting here for ages.*
Porter: *Which train, sir?*
Mr Grey: *The 8.18 to Baker Street.*
Porter: *The 8.18? I'm afraid you've made a mistake, sir.*
Mr Grey: *A mistake? My timetable says: Baker Street train – 8.18.*
Porter: *Oh no, sir. The Baker Street train leaves at 8.08.*
Mr Grey: *At 8.08?*
Porter: *You see, sir, they changed the timetable at the end of April. It's the first of May today.*
Mr Grey: *Changed it? May I see the new timetable? What does it say?*
Porter: *It says: Baker Street train – 8.08.*
Mr Grey: *Hm! So the train isn't late. I'm late.*

Intonation

Surprise

I'm afraid you've made *a mistake*, sir.

A *mistake*?

Listen and repeat:

The *eighth*?   By *plane*?

Today?   Going a*way*?

49

To *Spain*?   She's eighty-*eight*?

Practise in pairs.

Example:

It's *the eighth* of April.
A: It's the eighth of April.
B: The eighth?

1 It's *the eighth* of May.
2 Yes. It's Mrs Grey's birthday *today*.
3 Yes. She's *eighty-eight*.
4 Yes. And she's *going away* for a holiday.
5 That's right. And she's going *by plane*.
6 Well, it's a bit dangerous at her age, but she wants to go *to
   Spain*.
7 That's right. Why don't *you* go with her?

Unit 16 aɪ fine

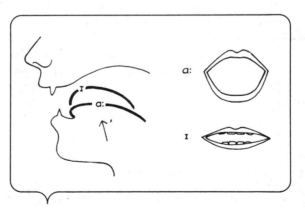

This has two sounds: ɑː and ɪ.
First practise the sound ɑː (see page 19)
This is a long sound.
Now add ɪ (see page 6).
This is a short sound.
aɪ.

50

Practice 1   Listen and repeat:

	sound 1	sound 2
	bar	buy
	star	sty
	darn	dine
	lark	like
	cart	kite
	heart	height

51

Unit 16   aɪ (fine)

Test   Tick the words you recognise in the sentences you hear:
1 a) cart; b) kite
2 a) darning; b) dining
3 a) star; b) sty
4 a) laugh; b) life
5 a) hard; b) hide
6 a) Pa; b) pie

Practice 2   Listen and repeat:

I'm	Myra	ice	tonight
'Bye	Violet	nice	all right
time	riding	like	type
mind	climbing	Mike	typist
Miles	ninety-nine	Nigel	typewriter

Dialogue # Mike, Myra and Violet

(Myra and Violet are typists in the library.)
Myra: (smiling) *Hello, Mike!*
Mike: *Hello, Myra. Hello, Violet! You're looking nice, Violet.*
(silence)
Mike: *Would you like some ice-cream, Violet?*
Violet: *No thanks, Mike. I'm busy typing. Talk to me some other time. I have ninety-nine pages to type by Friday.*
Mike: *Never mind. Do you like riding, Violet?*
Violet: *Sometimes.*
Mike: *Would you like to come riding with me tonight, Violet?*
Violet: *Not tonight, Mike. I'm going for a drive with Nigel.*
Mike: *What about Friday?*
Violet: *I'm going climbing with Miles.*
Mike: *Hm! Oh, all right. 'Bye!*
Myra: *Violet, he's put something behind your typewriter.*
Violet: *Is it something nice, Myra?*
Myra: *No. It's a spider.*

Conversation   Practise the words below, then use them in the dialogue in pairs.

flying   **ice** skating
driving   **horse** riding
climbing   **bic**ycle riding

A : Do you like . . . . ?
B : Yes. It's quite exciting.
A : Would you like to come . . . . with me on Friday?
B : Not Friday. Some other time.

Unit 17   ɔɪ   boy

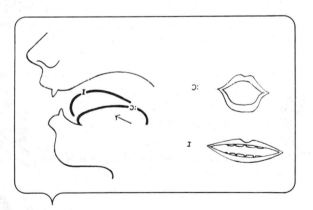

This has two sounds: ɔ: and ɪ (see pages 27 and 6).
First say ɔ:
Now make it longer: ɔɔɔ.
Then add ɪ. This is very short.
ɔɔɔɪ.

53

Practice 1   Listen and repeat:

   **sound 1**   **sound 2**

                         all   oil

   ball   boil

   corn   coin

                        tore   toy

   jaw   Joy

54

Test Tick the words you recognise in the sentences you hear:

1. a) corn; b) coin   4 a) aw; b) oi
2. a) bawling; b) boiling   5 a) bore; b) boy
3. a) all; b) oil   6 a) all; b) oil

Practice 2 Listen and repeat:

toy	annoying	Joyce
enjoy	boiling	voice
noisiest	pointing	Rolls Royce
destroyed	spoilt	boyfriend

Dialogue ## Joyce's Rolls Royce

(Joyce takes her Rolls Royce to the garage.)

Garage boy: *What a terrible noise.*

Joyce: *Eh?*

Garage boy: (raising his voice) WHAT A TERRIBLE NOISE! *This is the noisiest Rolls Royce I've ever heard.*

Joyce: (pointing) *It's out of oil.*

Garage boy: *Out of oil? And look! The water's boiling. Madam, a Rolls Royce isn't a toy. Perhaps you've spoilt the motor or even destroyed it.*

Joyce: *How annoying! While you're changing the oil, I'll go and visit my boyfriend, Roy.*

Stress Listen and repeat:

a loud **voice**
a spoilt **boy**
an awful **noise**
a noisy **toy**
an annoying **voice**

Practise in pairs:

Example:

A: That voice is very loud, isn't it?
B: Yes, it's a loud voice.

1 That boy is very spoilt.

55

2 That noise is really awful.
3 That toy is very noisy.
4 That boy is very noisy.
5 That noise is very annoying.

Unit 18 Review

I	2	3
eɪ	aɪ	ɔɪ
bay	buy	boy
ale	isle	oil
paint	pint	point
race	rice	Royce

Listening practice When you hear one of these words or sounds, say which number it is.

  Examples:

aɪ
Students: sound 2

boy
Students: sound 3

Reading   A painting of a boy

Jay: *Do you like painting?*

Joy: *Yes. I'm trying to paint a boy lying beside a lake. Do you like it?*

Jay: *Hm ... Why don't you buy some oil paints?*

Joy: *I don't enjoy painting with oils.*

Jay: *Your painting is quite nice, but why are you painting the boy's face grey?*

Joy: *(pointing) It isn't grey. It's white.*

Unit 19   aʊ   house

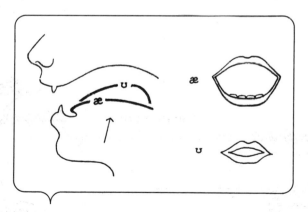

This has two sounds.
First practise the sound æ (see page 12).
Now add ʊ (see page 31). This is very short.
aʊ.

57

Practice 1 Listen and repeat:

	sound 1	sound 2	

car   cow

bar   bow

bra   brow

grass   grouse

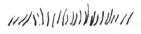

arch   ouch

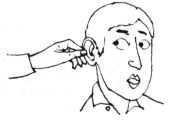

Unit 19   aʊ (house)

Test   Tick the words you recognise in the sentences you hear:

1 a) car; b) cow
2 a) grass; b) grouse
3 a) bra, b) brow
4 a) ha; b) how
5 a) ah; b) ow!
6 a) tarn; b) town

Practice 2   Listen and repeat:

Ow!	ground	out	our
now	Brown	mouse	ours
town	lounge	house	our house
found	loudly	shouting	
round	upside-down	couch	

Dialogue   A mouse in the house

Mrs Brown: (shouting loudly) I'VE FOUND A MOUSE!

Mr Brown: *Ow! You're shouting too loudly. Sit down and don't shout.*

Mrs Brown: (sitting down) *I've found a mouse in the house.*

Mr Brown: *A brown mouse?*

Mrs Brown: *Yes. A little round mouse. It's running around in the lounge.*

Mr Brown: *On the ground?*

Mrs Brown: *Yes. It's under the couch now.*

Mr Brown: *Well, get it out.*

Mrs Brown: *How?*

Mr Brown: *Turn the couch upside-down. Get it out somehow. We don't want a mouse in our house. Ours is the cleanest house in the town!*

Stress

Example 1:

Sit down.

Listen and repeat:
1 He's **sit**ting **down**.
2 He's **ly**ing **down**.
3 He's **stand**ing **up**.
4 He's **turn**ing **round**.
5 He's **shout**ing **out**.
6 He's **run**ning a**round**.

Match these pictures with the correct numbers:

a)   b)    c)

d)    e)    f)

Example 2:

Get it **out**.

Listen and repeat:
1 **Put** it **down**.
2 **Take** it **out**.
3 **Throw** it **out**.
4 **Turn** it **down**.
5 **Work** it **out**.

60

Match these pictures with the correct numbers:

a)   b)   c)

d)   e)

$15 + 73\frac{1}{2} \div 3 =$

Unit 20   əʊ   phone

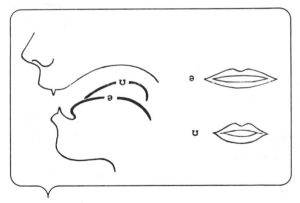

This has two sounds: ə and ʊ (see pages 42 and 31).
First say ə.
Now make it longer: əəə.
Then add ʊ. This is very short.
əəəʊ.

Unit 20   əʊ (phone)

Practice 1   Listen and repeat:

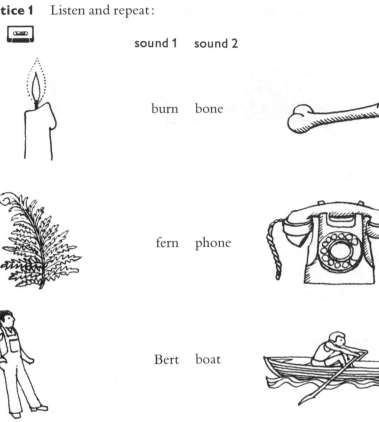

	sound 1	sound 2
	burn	bone
	fern	phone
	Bert	boat
	work	woke
	flirt	float

62

Practice 2 Listen and repeat:

sound 1   sound 2

caught   coat

nought   note

bought   boat

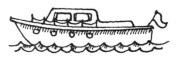

jaw   Joe

ball   bowl

63

Test Tick the words you recognise in the sentences you hear:

1 a) cork; b) coke
2 a) fern; b) phone
3 a) or; b) Oh!
4 a) ball; b) bowl
5 a) burn; b) bone
6 a) walk; b) work c) woke

Practice 3 Listen and repeat:

Oh!	know	don't	joking
no	throw	Joan	woke
Joe	snow	groans	coat
go	over	closed	OK
ago	nose	Jones	
window	hello	October	

Dialogue # Snow in October

(Joe Jones is sleeping, but Joan woke up a few minutes ago.)

Joan: *Joe! Joe! JOE! Hello!*
Joe: (groans) *Oh! What is it, Joan?*
Joan: *Look out of the window.*
Joe: *No. My eyes are closed, and I'm going to go to sleep again.*
Joan: *Don't go to sleep, Joe. Look at the snow!*
Joe: *Snow? But it's only October. I know there's no snow.*
Joan: *Come over to the window, Joe.*
Joe: *You're joking, Joan. There's no snow.*
Joan: *OK. I'll put my coat on and go out and make a snowball and throw it at your nose, Joe Jones!*

Practice 4 Listen and repeat:

old	hole	bowl
cold	hold	stole
sold	told	gold

In this list five words rhyme with 'old', and two words rhyme with 'hole'. Which words are they?

Rhyming crossword   The clues are words which rhyme with the answer but do not have the same meaning.

Clues

Across:	Down:
1 only	1 slow
2 don't	2 John
3 know	3 snow
4 Joe	4 no
5 billow	5 hello

Unit 21 Review

1	2
aʊ	əʊ
Ow!	Oh!
now	no
found	phoned
loud	load
about	a boat

Listening practice   When you hear one of these words or sounds, say which number it is.

   Examples:

əʊ	now
Students: sound 2	Students: sound 1

Reading The Jones's house

Mr Brown: *Excuse me. Do you know where the Jones's house is?*
An old man: *Yes. It's over that mountain along a very narrow road.*
Mr Brown: *Oh. Is it outside the town?*
Old man: *Yes. It's south of the town. You go past the hotel. The Jones's house has brown windows, and there are yellow roses growing round the windows.*

Unit 22 ɪə beer

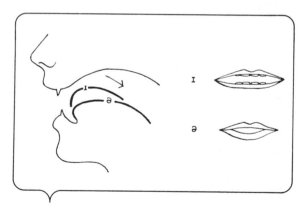

This has two sounds: ɪ and ə (see pages 6 and 42).
First make the sound ɪ.
Now add ə.
ɪə.

Practice 1   Listen and repeat:

sound 1   sound 2

   E   ear

   bee   beer

   tea   tear

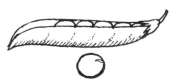   pea   pier

   bead   beard

Test   Tick the words you recognise in the sentences you hear:
1 a) bee; b) beer
2 a) tea; b) tear
3 a) bead; b) beard
4 a) pea; b) pier
5 a) E's; b) ears
6 a) Dee; b) dear

Practice 2   Listen and repeat:

Lear	year	Cheers!	Austria
here	idea	nearly	windier
hear	atmosphere	bearded	easier
dear	mountaineer	disappeared	
clear			

Dialogue   # A bearded mountaineer

(Mr and Mrs Lear are on holiday in Austria.)

Mr Lear: *Let's have a beer here, dear.*

Mrs Lear: *What a good idea! They have very good beer here. We came here last year.*

Mr Lear: *The atmosphere here is very clear.*

Mrs Lear: *And it's windier than last year.*

Mr Lear: (speaking to the waiter) *Two beers, please.*

Mrs Lear: *Look, dear! Look at that mountaineer drinking beer.*

Mr Lear: *His beard is in his beer.*

Mrs Lear: *His beard has nearly disappeared into his beer!*

Mr Lear: *Sh, dear! He might hear.*

Waiter: (bringing the beer) *Here you are, sir. Two beers.*

Mr Lear: (drinking his beer) *Cheers, dear!*

Mrs Lear: *Cheers! Here's to the bearded mountaineer!*

Joining words

'r' not pronounced	'r' pronounced
Listen and repeat:	Listen and repeat:
Here they are.	Here are all the books.
Here's the beer.	The beer is here on the table.
I can hear Mr Lear.	He can hear us too.
Mr Lear calls her 'dear'.	Dear old Mrs Lear is here in the kitchen.
He's a mountaineer.	A mountaineer always drinks beer in the mountains.

Unit 23 eə chair

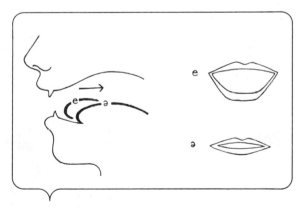

This has two sounds.
First practise the sound e (see page 9).
Now make it longer.
Now add ə (see page 42).
eə.

69

Practice 1   Listen and repeat:

	sound 1	sound 2	
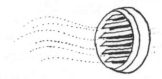	ear	air	
	beer	bear	
	pier	pear	
	hear	hair	
	tear	tear	
	Cheers!	chairs	

Test Tick the words you recognise in the sentences you hear:

1 a) cheers; b) chairs
2 a) beer; b) bear
3 a) pier; b) pear
4 a) here; b) hair
5 a) dear; b) Dare
6 a) clear; b) Claire

Practice 2 Listen and repeat:

Claire	there	nowhere
pair	they're	anywhere
chair	wearing	everywhere
square	Mary	upstairs and downstairs
where	hairbrushes	carefully

Dialogue # A pair of hairbrushes

Mary: *I've lost two small hairbrushes, Claire. They're a pair.*
Claire: *Have you looked carefully everywhere?*
Mary: *Yes. They're nowhere here.*
Claire: *Have you looked upstairs?*
Mary: *Yes. I've looked everywhere upstairs and downstairs. They aren't anywhere.*
Claire: *Hm! Are they square, Mary?*
Mary: *Yes. They're square hairbrushes. Have you seen them anywhere?*
Claire: *Well, you're wearing one of them in your hair!*
Mary: *Oh! Then where's the other one?*
Claire: *It's over there under the chair.*

Joining words

'r' not pronounced	'r' pronounced
Listen and repeat:	Listen and repeat:
Claire	Claire and Mary.
a pair	a pair of shoes
a square chair	a square envelope
It's there.	There it is.
They're here.	They're under a table.
I've looked everywhere for them.	I've looked everywhere in the house.

71

Section B

Vocabulary

First learn the words you will need in order to study how to make the sounds in this section:

Your mouth

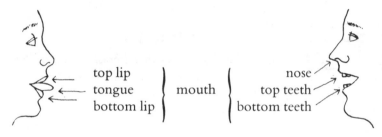

Practise:

		top lip		
		top teeth		
1	Touch your	bottom lip	with your finger.
		bottom teeth		
		tongue		
		nose		

2 Open your lips.   Close your lips.   Close your lips hard.

Inside your mouth

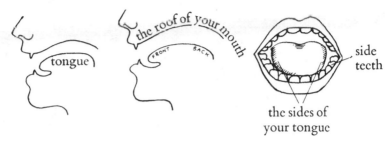

tongue

side teeth

the sides of your tongue

Practise:

1 Touch | your top teeth / your bottom teeth / the roof of your mouth | with your tongue.

2 Touch your side teeth with the sides of your tongue.

3 Touch the front of the roof of your mouth with the front of your tongue.

Touch the back of the roof of your mouth with the back of your tongue.

Air

1 Hold a piece of paper in front of your mouth.

When you blow out air the paper moves.

Air is coming through your mouth.

2 Close your mouth.   Push air forward in your mouth.

Voice

| Put your hand on the front of your neck. | When you sing you can feel your voice. You are using your voice. | The sound from your voice is coming through your mouth. |

  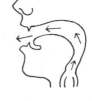

Unit 24   p   pen

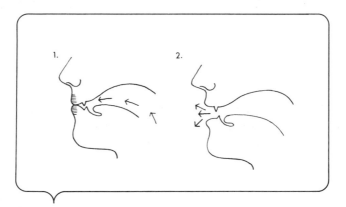

 1 Close your lips hard.
Push air forward in your mouth.
2 Then open your lips quickly.

74

Unit 24   **p** (pen)

Practice 1   Listen and repeat:

a pen   a pencil   a pin   a pear

Peter   Poppy   Paris

a pocket   a postcard   a passport

a passenger   a policeman   a newspaper

a pepper pot   a spoon   a piece of pork pie

an airport

stupid
impatient

Unit 24   **p** (pen)

a plane

a plastic plate

an apple, please

people

pretty
surprise

Practice 2   Listen and repeat.

The sound **p** is quieter in these words:

a cup

a pipe

an envelope

a stamp

Help!

Practice 3   Listen and repeat.

The sound **p** is very quiet in these words:

empty	upstairs	dropped	help me
helpful	perhaps	Mr Tupman	stop shouting
stop talking	stop pulling		

Dialogue   Passports, please

(Mr and Mrs Tupman are at the airport. They have just got off
the plane from Paris.)

Official:	*Passports, please!*
Mr Tupman:	*I think I've lost the passports, Poppy.*
Mrs Tupman:	*How stupid of you, Peter! Didn't you put them in your pocket?*
Mr Tupman:	(emptying his pockets) *Here's a pen ... a pencil ... my pipe ...a postcard ... an envelope ... a stamp ... a pin ...*
Mrs Tupman:	*Oh, stop taking things out of your pockets. Perhaps you put them in the plastic bag.*
Mr Tupman:	(emptying the plastic bag) *Here's a newspaper ... an apple ... a pear ... a plastic cup ... a spoon ... some paper plates ... a piece of pork pie ... a pepper pot ...*
Mrs Tupman:	*Oh, stop pulling things out of the plastic bag, Peter. These people are getting impatient.*
Mr Tupman:	*Well, help me, Poppy.*
Mrs Tupman:	*We've lost our passports. Perhaps we dropped them on the plane.*
Official:	*Then let the other passengers past, please.*
Mr Tupman:	*Poppy, why don't you help? You aren't being very helpful. Put the things in the plastic bag.*
Official:	*Your name, please?*
Mr Tupman:	*Tupman.*
Official:	*Please go upstairs with this policeman, Mr Tupman.*

Intonation   Listen and repeat:

He bought a p͡e̖n.

He bought a p͡e̖n and a p͡e̖ncil.

He bought a p͡e̖n and a p͡e̖ncil and a p͡i̗n.

Game   Peter went to Paris

Example:
A: Peter went to Paris, and he bought a pipe.
B: Peter went to Paris, and he bought a pipe and a picture.

Each student adds something to the list, and you must remember what the other students have said. Practise the game first with the class then in groups of five or six people. Practise the words in the list before you start, and try to use other words of your own with the sound **p** in them.

a newspaper	a postcard	a picture
a spoon	an apple	a piano
a pipe	a pear	a carpet
a pork pie	a paper plate	some soap
a pepper pot	a pen	a puppy
a stamp	a pencil	a plastic spider
an envelope	a pin	an expensive present for Poppy

Unit 25 b baby

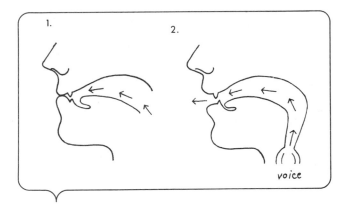

 First practise **p** (see page 74).
Use your voice to make **b**.

78

Practice 1   Listen and repeat:

	sound 1	sound 2	

     pin   bin   

   pen   Ben

     pear   bear   

   cap   cab   

   pup   pub   

     Poppy   Bobby

Unit 25   **b** (baby)

Test   Tick the words you recognise in the sentences you hear:

1 a) pin; b) bin
2 a) Poppy; b) Bobby
3 a) pup; b) pub
4 a) pig; b) big
5 a) pack; b) back
6 a) peach; b) beach

Practice 2   Listen and repeat:

Barbara	Ruby	black	brown
birthday	about	blue	brother
beautiful	remember	blouse	hairbrush
butterfly	somebody	terribly	Bob

Dialogue   # Happy birthday

Bob: *Hello, Barbara.*
Barbara: *Hello, Bob. It's my birthday today.*
Bob: *Oh, yes! Your birthday! Happy birthday, Barbara!*
Barbara: *Thanks, Bob. Somebody gave me this blouse for my birthday.*
Bob: *What a beautiful blouse! It's got brown and blue butterflies on it.*
Barbara: *And big black buttons.*
Bob: *Did Ruby buy it for you?*
Barbara: *Yes. And my brother gave me a hairbrush and a book about baby birds.*
Bob: *I didn't remember your birthday, Barbara. I'm terribly sorry.*
Barbara: *Well, you can buy me a big bottle of perfume, Bob!*
Bob: *I've got a better idea. We'll get into a cab and go to a pub, and I'll buy you a bottle of beer!*

Unit 25 b (baby)

Stress   Listen and repeat:

1 a **shelf**   a **book**shelf
2 a **brush**   a **hair**brush   a **paint**brush
3 a **card**   a **post**card   a **birth**day card
4 a **ball**   a **foot**ball   a **ping** pong ball
5 a **bag**   a **hand**bag   a **shopp**ing bag
6 a **man**   a po**lice**man   a **post**man

Conversation   Do this in pairs. Talk about these pictures. Follow the
example.

Example:

shelf

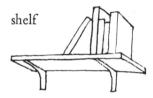

A: That's a shelf.
B: Yes, it's a bookshelf.

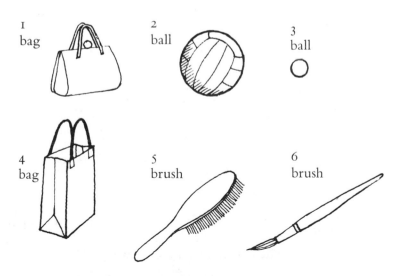

1
bag

2
ball

3
ball

4
bag

5
brush

6
brush

81

7
card

8
card

9
man

10
man

Unit 26 t tin

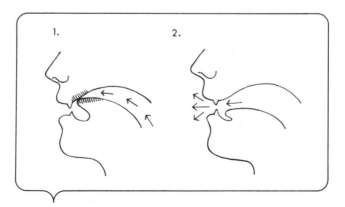

  1 Put the front of your tongue behind your top teeth. Push air
forward in your mouth.
2 Then move your tongue away.

Practice 1   Listen and repeat:

tin

tennis

cafeteria

fourteen

thirteen

top

tell the time
ten to ten

telephone

photographer

tomato

restaurant

pretty assistant

steak

student

upstairs

Practice 2   Listen and repeat.

'␣' is quieter in these words:

hat   coat   skirt

shirt   cricket bat

let   first
lift   basement
left

Practice 3   Listen and repeat.

'␣' is also quiet in these words:

travel	bootlace	hats
try	bottle	coats
lavatory	little	skirts
twenty	gentleman	shirts
twelve	exactly	restaurants
twins		cricket bats
department store		
want some	first floor	
fat man	light bulbs	
hot meal	fruit juice	

Dialogue   ## In a department store

Pretty girl:	*I want to buy a*	*hat.*
		coat.
		skirt.
		shirt.

Assistant:	*Hats*	*are upstairs on the*	*next*	*floor.*
	Coats		*first*	
	Skirts			
	Shirts			

Fat man: *Where can I get a hot meal?*

| Assistant: | *The* | *restaurant* | *is on the thirteenth floor.* |
| | | *cafeteria* | |

Little girl:	*I want to buy some*	*bootlaces*
		light bulbs.
		bottles of fruit juice.

Assistant: *They're on the next counter on your left, dear.*

| Tall lady: | *I want some tins of* | *tomato paste.* |
| | | *steak.* |

Assistant: *Try the supermarket in the basement.*

| Gentleman: | *Could you tell me where the* | *travel agency* | *is?* |
| | | *lavatory* | |

| Assistant: | *It's right next to the* | *cafeteria* | *on the thirteenth* |
| | | *restaurant* | *floor.* |

Student:	*I want to buy a*	*football.*
		cricket bat.
		tennis racquet.

Assistant:	*Take the lift to the sports department. It's on*	
	the	*top*	*floor.*
		fourteenth	

Little boy: *Could you tell me where the telephone is?*

Assistant: *It's on the twelfth floor opposite the photographer's.*

Twins: *Could you tell us the time, please?*

Assistant: *Yes. It's exactly twenty–two minutes to ten.*

Conversation Re-read the dialogue, then practise in pairs:

Example:

A: Could you tell me where the *restaurant* is?
B: Yes. It's on the thirteenth floor.

Use these words:

re**st**aurant   **tel**ephone   **lav**atory   **trav**el agency
sports department   **toil**et   cafe**ter**ia   pho**tog**rapher's

---

Unit 27 d   door

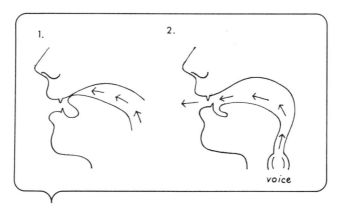

First practise t (see page 82).
Use your voice to make d.

Practice 1   Listen and repeat:

	sound 1	sound 2	

tore   door

tarts   darts

cart   card

write   ride

train   drain

trunk   drunk

Unit 27 d (door)

Test Tick the words you recognise in the sentences you hear:
1 a) writing; b) riding   4 a) sent; b) send
2 a) cart; b) card   5 a) tarts; b) darts
3 a) bat; b) bad   6 a) try; b) dry

Practice 2 Listen and repeat:

do	told	did	Sidney
date	tried	David	didn't
Daisy	rained	Donald	cards
Dotty	stayed	decided	bad cold
darling	studied	damaged	children
dancing	repaired		goodbye

Dialogue # A damaged telephone

Daisy: *Dunston 238282.*
Donald: *Hello, Daisy. This is Donald.*
Daisy: *Oh, hello, darling.*
Donald: *What did you do yesterday, Daisy? You forgot our date, didn't you?*
Daisy: *Well, it rained all day, Donald, and I have a bad cold, so I decided to stay at home.*
Donald: *Did you? I telephoned twenty times and nobody answered.*
Daisy: *Oh, the telephone was damaged. They repaired it today.*
Donald: *What did David do yesterday? Did he and Dotty go dancing?*
Daisy: *No. They stayed at home and played cards with the children.*
Donald: *And what did you do? Did you play cards too?*
Daisy: *No. Sidney and I listened to the radio and studied. What did you do yesterday, Donald?*
Donald: *I've just told you, Daisy. I tried to phone you twenty times!*

Pronunciation -ed endings

Listen and repeat:

ed = d	*ed* = t	*ed* = ɪd
play*ed*	brush*ed*	wait*ed*
clean*ed*	laugh*ed*	paint*ed*

88

snow*ed*	push*ed*	shout*ed*
clos*ed*	watch*ed*	want*ed*
fill*ed*	danc*ed*	land*ed*
stud*ied*	walk*ed*	depart*ed*

Conversation   Talk about these photographs:

Example:

studied all night
listened to the radio

He studied all night, didn't he?
No, he didn't. He listened to the radio.

1	2	3	4
			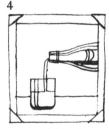
combed his hair brushed it	cried a lot laughed a lot	painted a room cleaned it	emptied his glass filled it

5	6	7	8

closed a door opened it	walked away waited a long time	washed the TV watched it	pulled his car pushed it

89

9

10

11

12

departed at noon
landed

whispered it
shouted it

danced all night
played cards

rained all day
snowed

Unit 28   k   key

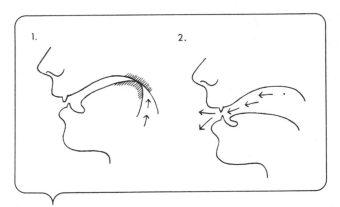

1. 2.

1 Touch the back of the roof of your mouth with the back of your tongue.
  Push air forward in your mouth.
2 Then move your tongue away.

90

Practice 1   Listen and repeat:

car   carpet   cuckoo

cup of coffee   American   ticket

pocket   school   scarf

scooter   sky   of course
                             because

Practice 2   Listen and repeat.

k is usually quieter here:

| like | look | milk | plastic |
| talk | work | ask | |

Practice 3   Listen and repeat.
k is usually very quiet here:

black dog	electric	book shelf	looked
take two	picture	asked	talked
cake fork	exactly	worked	

Practice 4

Listen and repeat:

Clark	six	cakes	quiet
clock	next	forks	quick
clever	exciting	clocks	quickly
cream	expensive	likes	question
cricket	excuse me	talks	thank you

Dialogue

The cuckoo clock

Mrs Cook: *Would you like some cream in your coffee, Mrs Clark?*

Mrs Clark: *No thank you. But I'd like a little milk.*

Mrs Cook: *Would you like some chocolate cakes?*

Mrs Clark: *Thank you.*

Mrs Cook: *Take two. Here's a cake fork, and here's a . . .*

Mrs Clark: *Excuse me, Mrs Cook. But what's that next to your bookshelf? Is it a clock?*

Mrs Cook: *Yes. It's an American cuckoo clock.*

Mrs Clark: *Is it plastic?*

Mrs Cook: *Oh, no, Mrs Clark. It's a very expensive clock. It's an electric clock.*

Mrs Clark: *Well, it's exactly six o'clock now, and it's very quiet. Doesn't it say 'cuckoo'?*

Mrs Cook: *Of course, Mrs Clark. Look!*

Clock: *Cuckoo! Cuckoo! Cuckoo! Cuckoo! Cuckoo! Cuckoo!*

Mrs Clark: *How exciting! What a clever clock!*

Clock: *Cuckoo!*

Stress

Listen and repeat:

1 a **clean shelf**   a clean **book**shelf
2 a **clean glass**   a clean **whis**ky glass
3 a **black cup**   a black **coff**ee cup
4 a **plas**tic **ring**   a plastic **key** ring
5 a **dirty bott**le   a dirty **coke** bottle
6 an e**lec**tric **clock**   an electric **cuck**oo clock
7 an ex**pen**sive **cake**   an expensive **choc**olate cake

Game   Jumbled sentences

Do this in pairs.

Example:

 cup a **coff**ee black it's

A: What's this?
B: It's a black coffee cup.

1  an it's **cuck**oo electric clock

2 ring plastic it's **key** a

3   **whis**ky dirty it's glass a

4  it's bottle dirty a **coke**

5  expensive cake **cream** an it's

93

6

it's **car** comfortable coat a

7

book black a it's add**ress**

8

it's collector drunk a **tick**et

Unit 29   g   girl

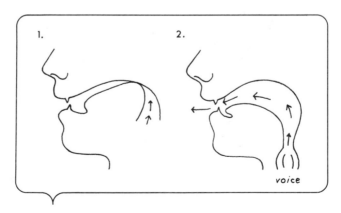

First practise **k** (see page 90).
Use your voice to make **g**.

Practice 1   Listen and repeat:

	sound 1	sound 2	
	cold	gold	
	coat	goat	
	curl	girl	
	class	glass	
	back	bag	
	clock	clog	

Test Tick the words you recognise in the sentences you hear:

1 a) cold; b) gold
2 a) back; b) bag
3 a) clock; b) clog
4 a) curl; b) girl
5 a) frock; b) frog
6 a) clue; b) glue

Practice 2 Listen and repeat:

give	guests	August	Greek
beginning	garden	guitar	Margaret
get	gun	dog	telegram
together	good	Craig	glad
again	go	Greg	England

Dialogue ## Guests in August

Craig: *I've just got a telegram from Margaret and Greg.*
Carol: *Are they coming to England again?*
Craig: *Yes. At the beginning of August.*
Carol: *Good. We can all get together again.*
Craig: *I'm glad they're coming in August. We can take the dog and go for walks together.*
Carol: *Yes. And we can give a garden party.*
Craig: *And Margaret can play her guitar in the garden and sing Greek songs again.*
Carol: *Yes. August is a good time to come to England.*

Stress This is the telegram from Margaret and Greg:
ARRIVING ENGLAND BEGINNING AUGUST
and this is what it means:
We're arriving in England at the beginning of August.
This is much longer, but try to say both sentences in the same length of time. Listen and repeat:
a**rriv**ing **Eng**land be**ginn**ing **Aug**ust
We're a**rriv**ing in **Eng**land at the be**ginn**ing of **Aug**ust.

Now try these:
1 **Glad com**ing **Aug**ust
  We're **glad** you're **com**ing in **Aug**ust.

2 **Bring gun, golf clubs**
  Bring your **gun** and your **golf clubs**.

3 **Bring** guitar
  Bring your guitar.

4 **Lost** guitar. **Send cash**
  I've **lost** my guitar. Could you **send** me some **cash**?

5 For**get** guitar. Bring gun
  For**get** about your gui**tar** but **bring** your **gun**.

Unit 30   s   sun

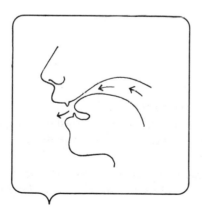

Touch your side teeth with the sides of your tongue.
Put your tongue forward.
Do not use your voice.

Practice 1   Listen and repeat:

Sue    bus    said

piece    sip 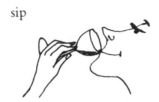   price

Practice 2   Listen and repeat:

sit	sensible	interesting	sleep	six
Sam	outside	instead	spend	yes
sand	seaside	just	swim	Alice
Saturday		star	skiing	
Sunday		it's	expensive	
sailing		let's	exciting	

Dialogue   ## It's expensive

Sam: *Let's go to the seaside on Saturday.*

Alice: *Yes! Let's go sailing and water-skiing. That's exciting.*

Sam: *It's expensive too. Let's just sit in the sun and go swimming instead.*

Alice: *Let's stay in the Six Star Hotel and spend Sunday there too.*

Sam: *Be sensible, Alice. It's too expensive. Let's sleep outside instead.*

Alice: *Yes. Let's sleep on the sand. That's more exciting.*

Unit 30   s (sun)

Joining   Listen and repeat:
sounds   Let's sit in the sun.

   Let's stay in a hotel.

Let's sleep outside.

Let's spend Sunday there too.

Six Star.

He smokes cigarettes.

He wants some books.

He speaks slowly.

Drill   Example: I like cats.
Answer: Sam likes cats too.

1 I hate hats.
2 I smoke cigarettes.
3 I eat biscuits.
4 I laugh at jokes.
5 I sit on seats.
6 I want some books.
7 I take photographs.
8 I get headaches.

Conversation   Practise in pairs.

Example:

A: Shall we go to the seaside or stay at home?
B: Let's │ go to the seaside.
        │ stay at home.

1 Shall we take a suitcase or a basket?
2 Shall we go sailing or water-skiing?
3 Shall we sit in the sun or go swimming?
4 Shall we eat biscuits or ice-cream?
5 Shall we sit on a seat or sit on the sand?
6 Shall we sleep outside or in an expensive hotel?
7 Shall we be sensible or silly?

99

Reading Practise reading aloud:

 ## The smile of a snake

She speaks slowly, and smokes special, expensive cigarettes. As she steps upstairs, her long skirt sweeps over her silver slippers. She is small and smart and sweet-smelling. Her skin is like snow.

'You have stolen my heart!' I once said stupidly, and she smiled. But when she smiled, she smiled the smile of a snake.

Unit 31 z zoo

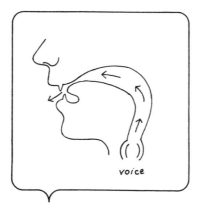

voice

 First practice s (see page 97).
Use your voice to make z.

Practice 1   Listen and repeat:

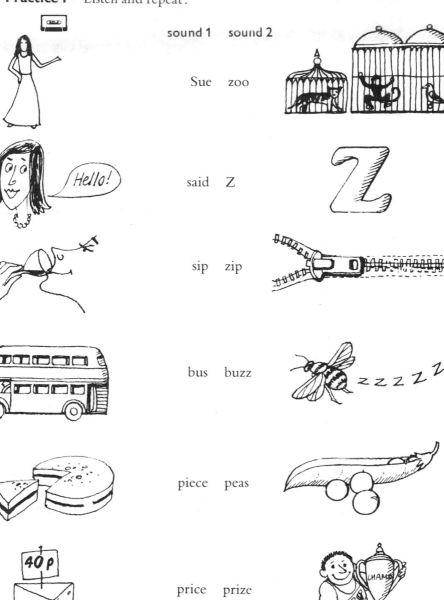

	sound 1	sound 2
	Sue	zoo
	said	Z
	sip	zip
	bus	buzz
	piece	peas
	price	prize

Unit 31   z (zoo)

Test

Tick the words you recognise in the sentences you hear:

1 a) bus; b) buzz   4 a) pence; b) pens
2 a) sip; b) zip   5 a) police; b) please
3 a) price; b) prize   6 a) Sackville; b) Zackville

Practice 2

Listen and repeat:

Zzz!	Mrs	hisses
zoo	these	smells
buzzing	bees	something's
surprising	is	contains
amazing	does	Jones
surprises	says	isn't
buzzes	noise	

Dialogue

Surprises in the post office

Mrs Smith: *This parcel smells, Mrs Jones.*
Mrs Jones: *Something's written on it.*
Mrs Smith: *What does it say?*
Mrs Jones: *It says: This parcel contains six mice.*
Mrs Smith: *Pooh!*
Mrs Jones: *Listen! What's in this sack?*
Mrs Smith: *It's making a strange hissing noise.*
Sack: *(hisses) Sssssssssssssss!*
Mrs Jones: *Mrs Smith! It's a sack of snakes!*
Mrs Smith: *So it is! And what's in this box, Mrs Jones?*
Mrs Jones: *It's making a buzzing sound.*
Box: *(buzzes) Zzzzzzzzzzzzzz!*
Mrs Smith: *These are bees!*
Mrs Smith: *A parcel of mice! And a sack of snakes! And a box of bees! This is very surprising.*
Mrs Jones: *It's amazing. This isn't a post office, Mrs Jones. It's a zoo!*

Drills

Example: I love dogs.
Answer: Susan loves dogs too.

1 I answer questions.
2 I listen to jazz records.
3 I climb mountains.

4 I need some scissors.
5 I buy expensive clothes.
6 I have six cousins.
7 I wear sun–glasses.
8 I always lose things.

Example: Does Sam always buy one rose?
Answer: No. He buys lots of roses.

1 Does Sam own just one horse?
2 Does Sam win just one prize?
3 Does Susan need only one dress?
4 Does your cousin use only one glass?
5 Does Susan wash just one blouse?
6 Does Sam pass just one house?
7 Does this student finish just one exercise?
8 Does Sam kiss only one nurse?

Unit 32 ∫ shoe

First practise **s** (see page 97).
Then put your tongue up and back a little to make ∫.

Practice 1   Listen and repeat:

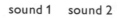

	sound 1	sound 2	

sea   she

   Sue   shoe

   sip   ship

ass   ash

   Russ   rush

   puss   push

Unit 32 ʃ (shoe)

Test Tick the words you recognise in the sentences you hear:

1 a) Sue's; b) shoes
2 a) ass; b) ash
3 a) puss; b) push
4 a) sack; b) shack
5 a) seats; b) sheets
6 a) save; b) shave 🔑

Practice 2 Listen and repeat:

sheets	Shaw	washing	Swedish
shall	shake	machine	English
shop	show	special	shrunk
shut	shirts	Marsh	finished
shouldn't	sure	wish	demonstration

Dialogue A special washing machine

Mrs Marsh: *Does this shop sell washing machines?*
Mr Shaw: *Yes. This is the newest washing machine, madam.*
Mrs Marsh: *Is it Swedish?*
Mr Shaw: *No, madam. It's English.*
Mrs Marsh: *Please show me how it washes.*
Mr Shaw: *Shall I give you a demonstration? Here are some sheets and shirts. You put them in the machine. You shut the door. And you push this button.*
Mrs Marsh: *The machine shouldn't shake like that, should it?*
Mr Shaw: *Washing machines always shake, madam. Ah! It's finished now.*
Mrs Marsh: *But the sheets have shrunk, and so have the shirts.*
Mr Shaw: *Do you wish to buy this machine, madam?*
Mrs Marsh: *I'm not sure.*

Joining sounds Listen and repeat:

English shops   *Irish sheets

Danish ships   *Polish shirts

Scottish sheep   *Finnish shorts

*Swedish shampoo   *Turkish sugar

*French champagne *Spanish shoes

Conversation   Customer: *Does this shop sell ★Swedish shampoo?*
Shop assistant: *Yes. We have some special Swedish shampoo on this shelf.*

Practise this conversation. Use the ★list above.

Unit 33   ʒ   television

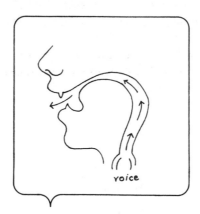

voice

First practise ʃ (see page 103).
Use your voice to make ʒ.

Practice 1   Listen and repeat:

 television

garage

measuring tape

Peugeot

treasure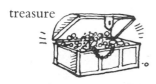

casual clothes

Asia

an unusual collision

Reading   Television programmes: Channel O

7.00 – Children's film: '*Treasure Island*'
7.15 – News comment: *An Unusual Collision*
7.30 – Fashion: *Casual Clothes*
7.45 – Travel film: *Across Asia in a Peugeot*
8.15 – Do-it-yourself: *How to Measure a New Garage*
8.30 – Variety show: *It's a Pleasure*

Conversation Talk about the television programmes.

Example:
A: What are you going to watch on television tonight?
B: Treasure Island.

Drill When somebody says 'Thank you' for doing something, we sometimes say, 'It's a pleasure'. Practise this answer.

Example:
A: Thank you for lending me your television.
B: It's a pleasure.

1 Thank you for mending my television.
2 Thanks for lending me your measuring tape.
3 Thanks for lending me 'Treasure Island'.
4 Thank you for letting me use your garage.
5 Thanks for letting me drive your Peugeot.
6 Thanks for letting us watch your television.

Unit 34 tʃ cherry

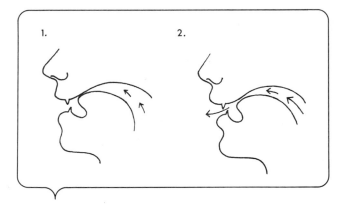

 First practise t and ʃ (see pages 82 and 103).
1 Begin to make t.
2 Then slowly move your tongue from the roof of your mouth.

Practice 1 Listen and repeat:

	sound 1	sound 2	
	ships	chips	
	sheep	cheap	
	sherry	cherry	
	shop	chop	
	cash	catch	
	wash	watch	

Test

Tick the words you recognise in the sentences you hear:

1 a) shop; b) chop
2 a) sherry; b) cherry
3 a) washing; b) watching
4 a) ships; b) chips
5 a) shin; b) chin
6 a) shoes; b) choose

Practice 2

Listen and repeat:

children	butcher's shop	Mrs Church
cheque	chump chops	much
Cheshire	shoulder chops	which
cheaper	a delicious chicken	
choose	children's lunch	

Dialogue

At the butcher's shop

Butcher: *Good morning, Mrs Church.*

Mrs Church: *Good morning, Mr Cheshire. I'd like some chops for the children's lunch.*

Butcher: *Chump chops or shoulder chops, Mrs Church?*

Mrs Church: *I'll have four shoulder chops, and I want a small chicken.*

Butcher: *Would you like to choose a chicken, Mrs Church?*

Mrs Church: *Which one is cheaper?*

Butcher: *This one's the cheapest. It's a delicious chicken.*

Mrs Church: *How much is all that? I haven't got cash. Can I pay by cheque?*

Butcher: *Of course, Mrs Church.*

Recipe

Cheese-topped chops

4 chops   sherry   Cheddar cheese

1 fresh chilli   mushrooms
or
a pinch of chilli
powder (not too
much chilli)

shallots

1

Pour a little sherry over the
chops.

2

Chop the mushrooms, cheese
and shallots.

3

Mix the mushrooms, cheese,
shallots and chilli.

4

Grill the chops.

5

Put the chops in a dish.

6

Spread the mixture over the
chops.

7

Grill the chops and mixture for a few minutes.

8

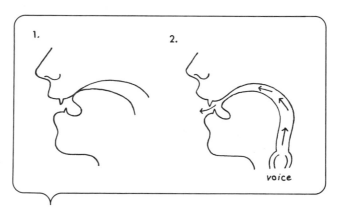

Serve the chops with fresh French salad and chips.

Unit 35 dʒ jam

1.

2.

voice

First practise tʃ (see page 108).
Use your voice to make dʒ.

Practice 1   Listen and repeat:

	sound 1	sound 2	
cheap	jeep	
choke	joke	
chin	gin	
cherry	Jerry	
larch	large	
H	age	

Unit 35   dʒ (jam)

Test   Tick the words you recognise in the sentences you hear:

1 a) choking; b) joking
2 a) larch; b) large
3 a) cheap; b) jeep
4 a) chain; b) Jane
5 a) chilly; b) Jilly
6 a) cheered; b) jeered   🗝

Practice 2   Listen and repeat:

gin	dangerous	village
jeep	manager	bridge
January	agency	edge
just	injured	large
joke	passenger	George Churchill
jail	damaged	ginger-haired chap

Dialogue   # George Churchill

Jerry: *Just outside this village there's a very dangerous bridge.*
John: *Yes. Charles told me two jeeps crashed on it in January. What happened?*
Jerry: *Well George Churchill was the driver of the larger jeep, and he was driving very dangerously. He'd been drinking gin.*
John: *George Churchill? Do I know George Churchill?*
Jerry: *Yes. That ginger-haired chap. He's the manager of the travel agency in Chester.*
John: *Oh, yes. I remember George. He's always telling jokes. Well, was anybody injured?*
Jerry: *Oh, yes. The other jeep went over the edge of the bridge, and two children and another passenger were badly injured.*
John: *Were both the jeeps damaged?*
Jerry: *Oh, yes.*
John: *And what happened to George?*
Jerry: *George? He's telling jokes in jail now, I suppose!*

**Joining
sounds**

When two sounds tʃ or d3 come together, you must say both
sounds. Listen and repeat:

orange juice	rich child	which job
village jail	watch chain	college chess
large gentleman	which chair	large cherries
huge jam-jar	how much cheese	teach German

Crossword Every answer has the sound tʃ or d3.

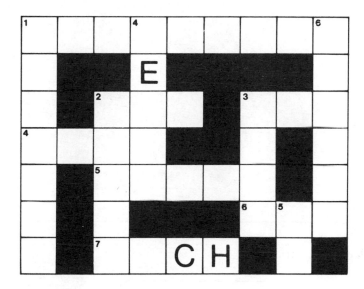

Clues

Across:
1 Famous English prime minister.
2 We eat bread, butter and ...
3 We buy jam in a ...
4 You'll get fat if you eat too much .... olate.
5 A game for two people.
6 You can see in the dark with a ... ch.
7 This isn't .... a difficult puzzle.

Down:
1 A young hen is a ....
2 This book belongs to Jock. It's ....'. book.

3 The dangerous bridge is .... outside the village.
4 HRCAE are letters of this word. It means get with your hand.
5 Tell me a j . . e.
6 George's jeep was . . . . . . than the other jeep.

Unit 36 f fan

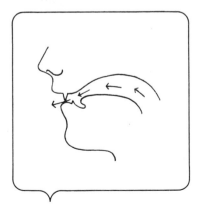

Touch your top teeth with your bottom lip.
Blow out air between your lip and your teeth.

Practice 1   Listen and repeat:

	sound 1	sound 2	

pin   fin

peel   feel

pail   fail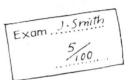

pine   fine

snip   sniff

harp   half

117

Practice 2   Listen and repeat:

	sound 1	sound 2	

   heat   feet

hat   fat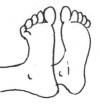

 hill   fill

 heel   feel

hall   fall

 hole   foal

Test   Tick the words you recognise in the sentences you hear:

1 a) pin; b) fin
2 a) peel; b) feel
3 a) snipping; b) sniffing
4 a) heel; b) feel
5 a) hat; b) fat
6 a) pole; b) hole; c) foal

Practice 3   Listen and repeat:

fill in	full front	comfortable	photograph
finished	friendly	after	photographer
feels fine	office	Mr Puffin	myself
five	sofa	difficult	soft
for	profile	if	Phillip
form	telephone	wife	Phillippa
February	beautiful	laugh	

Dialogue   # At the photographer's

Phillip: *I want a photograph of myself and my wife.*

Photographer: *Please fill in this form, sir.*
Would you prefer a full front photograph or a profile?

Phillip: *A full front, don't you think, Phillippa?*

Phillippa: *Yes. A full front photograph.*

Photographer: *Please sit on this sofa. Is it comfortable, Mrs Puffin?*

Phillippa: *Yes. It feels fine.*

Photographer: *Mr Puffin, please give a friendly laugh.*

Phillip: *That's difficult. If you say something funny I can laugh.*

Photographer: *And, Mrs Puffin, please look soft and beautiful.*

Phillip: (laughs)

Phillippa: *Is it finished?*

Photographer: *Yes.*

Phillip: *Will the photograph be ready for the first of February?*

Photographer: *Yes. Please phone my office after five days, Mr Puffin.*

Intonation   Listen and repeat:

If Fred **laughs**, he looks **fun**ny.

If Grandfather **flies**, he gets **fright**ened.

Jumbled   If Fred laughs,   he isn't free.
sentences   If Phillippa laughs,   he gets frightened.
                 If Grandfather flies,   she looks beautiful.
                 If you want to eat fish,   you're first.
                 If you telephone information,   it gets full of fat.
                 If you fry food,   they're helpful.
                 If a man has a wife,   he looks funny.
                 If you finish before the others,   you need a knife and fork.

Example:

If Fred laughs, he looks funny.

Unit 37   v   van

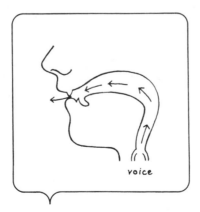

voice

First practise **f** (see page 116).
Use your voice to make **v**.

Practice 1   Listen and repeat:

	sound 1	sound 2	

	feel	veal	
	fine	vine	
	fail	veil	
	few	view	
	leaf	leave	
	half	halve	

121

Practice 2   Listen and repeat:

	sound 1	**sound 2**	
	bet	vet	
	best	vest	
	ban	van	
	bolts	volts	
	boat	vote	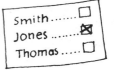
	bowl	vole	

Unit 37 v (van)

Test Tick the words you recognise in the sentences you hear:

1. a) few; b) view
2. a) half; b) halve
3. a) fast; b) vast
4. a) boat; b) vote
5. a) bolts; b) volts
6. a) fowls; b) bowels; c) vowels

Practice 3 Listen and repeat:

Vera	living	have
very	November	five
village	leaving	love
valley	driving	lovely
van	lived	leaves
Victor	arrived	

Dialogue ## A fine view

Vera: *Has your family lived here for very long?*
Victor: *Five and a half years. We arrived on the first of February.*
Vera: *What a fine view you have!*
Victor: *Yes. I love living here.*
Vera: *Look! You can see the village down in the valley.*
Victor: *Yes. It's a lovely view.*

Reading This is a photograph of a fat farmer arriving at a village in the valley. He's driving a van. It's a fine day, but it's November, and the leaves have fallen from the vine in the front of the photograph.

Unit 37   v (van)

Conversation   Ask somebody these questions about the photograph:
1 Who's driving the van?
2 How many leaves have fallen from the vine?
3 Where do the villagers live?
4 Is the van leaving or arriving?
5 Is it a vine or a fir tree in the front of the photograph?
6 Are there four or five fir trees near the village?

Unit 38   w   window

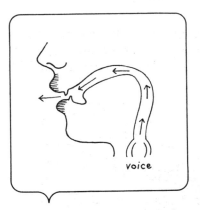

voice

First practise u: (see page 34). Make your lips round and hard for **w**.
w is a short sound.

Practice 1 Listen and repeat:

sound 1	sound 2
V	we
veal	wheel
vest	west
vet	wet
vine	wine
veil	whale

Unit 38   **w** (window)

Test   Tick the words you recognise in the sentences you hear:

1 a) vine; b) wine   4 a) verse; b) worse
2 a) V; b) we   5 a) veils; b) whales
3 a) veal; b) wheel   6 a) viper; b) wiper

Practice 2   Listen and repeat:

when	walk	were	twelve
well	warm	where	twenty
wet weather	wonderful	wore	quiet
Wendy went	woods	away	quickly
which	why	railway	sweet
what was	wild	everywhere	Gwen
watched	white wine	sandwiches	squirrels

Dialogue   # A walk in the woods

Gwen: *Did you see Victor on Wednesday, Wendy?*
Wendy: *Yes. We went for a walk in the woods near the railway.*
Gwen: *Wasn't it cold on Wednesday?*
Wendy: *Yes. It was very cold and wet. We wore warm clothes and walked quickly to keep warm.*
Gwen: *It's lovely and quiet in the woods.*
Wendy: *Yes. Further away from the railway it was very quiet, and there were wild squirrels everywhere. We counted twenty squirrels.*
Gwen: *How wonderful! Twenty squirrels! And did you take lunch with you?*
Wendy: *Yes. About twelve we had veal sandwiches and sweet white wine, and we watched the squirrels. It was a very nice walk.*

Intonation   Listen and repeat:

Where was it **qui**et?   In the **woods**.

What did they **drink**?   Sweet white **wine**.

Why did they walk **quick**ly?   To keep **warm**.

Jumbled   Ask somebody these questions about the dialogue:
answers

Where was it *quiet*?	The *squirrels*.
What did they *watch*?	In the *woods*.
What did they *drink*?	To keep *warm*.
Where were the *squirrels*?	Twelve o'*clock*.
Why did they walk *quickly*?	In the *woods*.
What did they eat for *lunch*?	They went for a *walk*.
What time did they have *lunch*?	Veal *sand*wiches.
What did Victor and Wendy do on	Sweet white *wine*.
*We*dnesday?	

Unit 39   j   yellow

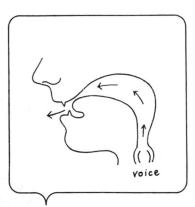

First practise i: (see page 3).
Very quickly move your tongue to make the next sound.
Do not touch the roof of your mouth with your tongue.

127

Practice 1   Listen and repeat:

	sound 1	sound 2

joke   yolk

Jack   yak

jam   yam

Jess   yes

jeers   years

Unit 39   j (ýellow)

Test Tick the words you recognise in the sentences you hear:

1 a) joke; b) yolk
2 a) jam; b) yam
3 a) Jess; b) yes
4 a) jeers; b) years
5 a) juice; b) use
6 a) jet; b) yet

Practice 2   Listen and repeat:

yes	millionaire	tubes	few
yesterday	you	stupid	knew
yellow	university	student	New York
years	excuse me	stew	music
York	tutor	Hugh	beautiful
Europe	tunes	huge	produces
onion	tuba	Young	

Dialogue

A stupid student

Jim: *Excuse me. Did you use to live in York?*
Jack: *Yes.*
Jim: *Did you use to be a tutor at the University?*
Jack: *Yes. For a few years.*
Jim: *Do you remember Hugh Young? He was a music student.*
Jack: *Hugh Young? Did he use to have a huge yellow jeep?*
Jim: *Yes. And he used to play beautiful tunes on the tuba.*
Jack: *Yes, I knew Hugh. He used to be a very stupid student. Do you have any news of Hugh?*
Jim: *Yes. He's a millionaire now in New York.*
Jack: *A millionaire? Playing the tuba?*
Jim: *Oh, no. He produces jam in tubes, and tins of sausages and onion stew, and sells them in Europe. I read about Hugh in the newspaper yesterday.*
Jack: *Oh! Well, he wasn't so stupid.*

Conversation   Practise in pairs:

Example:
wash yourself

A: When you were very young, did you use to wash
   yourself?
B: Yes I did. / No, I didn't.

1 dress yourself
2 feed yourself
3 be beautiful
4 be stupid
5 like music

Unit 40 h   hat

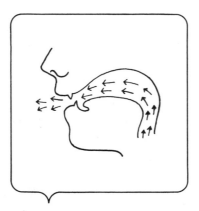

Push a lot of air out very quickly.
Do not touch the roof of your mouth with your tongue.

Practice 1   Listen and repeat:

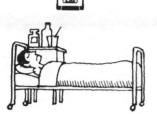

	sound 1 (no sound)	sound 2	
	ill	hill	
	eel	heel	
	and	hand	
	old	hold	
	ear	hear	
	eye	high	

131

Unit 40   h (hat)

Test Tick the words you recognise in the sentences you hear:

1 a) eels; b) heels
2 a) and; b) hand
3 a) eye; b) high
4 a) art; b) heart
5 a) ow; b) how
6 a) air; b) hair

Practice 2 Listen and repeat:

hit	having	horse
Hilda	happened	heard
Mrs Higgins	hospital	hope
hello	horrible	perhaps
Helen	how	behind
husband	house	unhappy

Dialogue # A horrible accident

Helen: *Hello, Ellen.*
Ellen: *Hello, Helen. Have you heard? There's been a horrible accident.*
Helen: *Oh, dear! What's happened?*
Ellen: *Hilda Higgins' husband has had an accident on his horse.*
Helen: *How awful! Is he injured?*
Ellen: *Yes. An ambulance has taken him to hospital.*
Helen: *How did it happen?*
Ellen: *He was hit by an express train. It was on the crossing just behind his house.*
Helen: *How horrible!*
Ellen: *He's having an important operation in hospital now. Poor Hilda! She's so unhappy.*
Helen: *Perhaps he'll be all right.*
Ellen: *I hope so.*

Intonation Listen and repeat:

Oh **dear**! How **horr**ible!

How **aw**ful! How **terr**ible!

132

Conversation   Practise in pairs:

Example:

A: Harold has had an accident.
B: How awful!

1 A helicopter has hit Allen's house.
2 Harry has a hole in his head.
3 Andrew spent all his holiday in hospital.
4 Hilda hit herself with a heavy hammer.
5 Ellen's husband is ill in hospital.
6 I've hurt my hand and I can't hold anything.

Unit 41   θ   thin

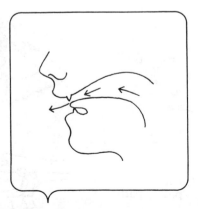

Put your tongue between your teeth.
Blow out air between your tongue and your top teeth.

133

Practice 1   Listen and repeat:

	sound 1	sound 2	

   mouse   mouth

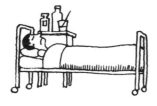   sum   thumb

   sick   thick

   sink   think

pass   path

Practice 2   Listen and repeat:

	sound 1	sound 2	

free   three

first   thirst

fin   thin

Fred   thread

half   hearth

Practice 3   Listen and repeat:

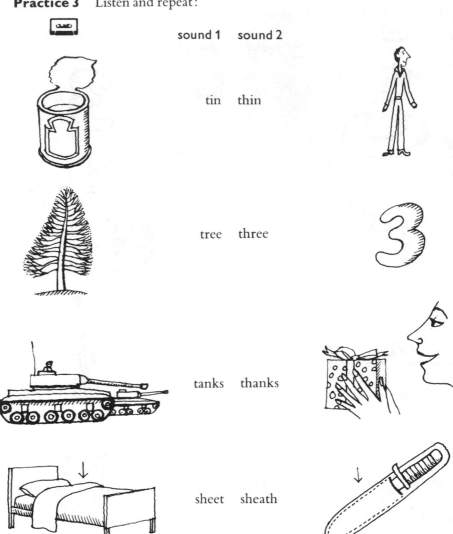

	sound 1	sound 2	
	tin	thin	
	tree	three	
	tanks	thanks	
	sheet	sheath	

Unit 41 θ (thin)

Test

Tick the words you recognise in the sentences you hear:
1 a) sink; b) think
2 a) mouse; b) mouth
3 a) tin; b) thin
4 a) taught; b) thought
5 a) moss; b) moth
6 a) fought; b) thought

Practice 4

Listen and repeat:

thank you	Ethel	Judith
thought	author	worth
thousand	nothing	Mrs Smith
thirsty	something	Smiths'
Thursday	birthday	Edith
thirty-three	mathematician	moths

Dialogue

Gossips

Judith: *Edith Smith is only thirty.*
Ethel: *Is she? I thought she was thirty-three.*
Judith: *Edith's birthday was last Thursday.*
Ethel: *Was it? I thought it was last month.*
Judith: *The Smiths' house is worth thirty thousand pounds.*
Ethel: *Is it? I thought it was worth three thousand.*
Judith: *Mr Smith is the author of a book about moths.*
Ethel: *Is he? I thought he was a mathematician.*
Judith: *I'm so thirsty.*
Ethel: *Are you? I thought you drank something at the Smiths'.*
Judith: *No. Edith gave me nothing to drink.*
Ethel: *Shall I buy you a drink?*
Judith: *Thank you.*

Stress

Listen and repeat:
Is she? I thought she was thirty-**three**.
Was it? I thought it was last **month**.
Is it? I thought it was worth **three** thousand.
Are you? I thought you **drank** something.

137

Jumbled
sentences

Do this in pairs.

Example:

A: Judith is at the theatre.

B Is she? I thought she was at the Smiths'.

A: Judith is at the theatre.
   Mr Smith is thirty-three.
   It's Edith's birthday today.
   I'm so thirsty.
   The Smiths' house is north.
   Mrs Smith is thirty.
   The Smiths' house is worth £30,000.

B: Are you? I thought you drank something.
   Is she? I thought she was at the Smiths'.
   Is he? I thought he was thirty.
   Is she? I thought she was thirty-three.
   Is it? I thought it was last month.
   Is it? I thought it was worth £3,000.
   Is it? I thought it was south.

Unit 42 ð the feather

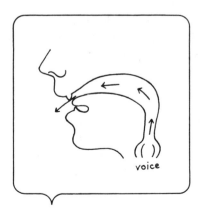

voice

First practise θ (see page 133). Use your voice to make ð.

Unit 42 ð (the feather)

Practice 1 Listen and repeat:

	sound 1	sound 2	

Dan   than

day   they

dare   there

doze   those

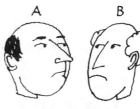

Ida   either

139

Practice 2   Listen and repeat.

Practise these questions and answers:

What's this?   This is the zoo.

What are those?   Those are zebras.

What's that?   That's a zebu.

What's this?   This is Z.

What's that?   That's zero.

What are these?   These are zips.

Who's that?   That's Zack.

140

Practice 3   Listen and repeat:

	sound 1	sound 2	
	bays	bathe	
	close	clothe	
	whizz	with	
	breeze	breathe	
	boos	booth	
	size	scythe	

Unit 42   ð (the feather)

Test   Tick the words you recognise in the sentences you hear:
1 a) Ida; b) either
2 a) day; b) they
3 a) dares; b) there's
4 a) size; b) scythe
5 a) bays; b) bathe
6 a) boos; b) booth

Practice 4   Listen and repeat:

the	together	another
this	feathers	smoother
that	leather	rather
clothes	Miss Brothers	

Dialogue   # The hat in the window

Miss Brothers: *I want to buy the hat in the window.*
Assistant: *There are three hats together in the window, madam. Do you want the one with the feathers?*
Miss Brothers: *No. The other one.*
Assistant: *The small one for three pounds?*
Miss Brothers: *No. Not that one either. That one over there. The leather one.*
Assistant: *Ah! The leather one.*
Now this is another leather hat, madam. It's better than the one in the window. It's a smoother leather.
Miss Brothers: *I'd rather have the one in the window. It goes with my clothes.*
Assistant: *Certainly, madam. But we don't take anything out of the window until three o'clock on Thursday.*

Stress   Listen and repeat:

Which hat do **you** think is **bett**er than the **oth**ers?
I think the **one** with the **feath**ers is **bett**er than the **oth**ers.

Conversation

Talk about the three hats using the words from the list below:

A: **Which hat** do **you** think is **bett**er than the **oth**ers?

B: I think the | one with the **feath**ers
leather **hat**
hat for **three pounds** | is ... than the **oth**ers.

better	more **fash**ionable
cheaper	more **stu**pid
prettier	more **com**fortable
uglier	more ex**pen**sive
tall **tall**	**won**

Unit 43 m   mouth

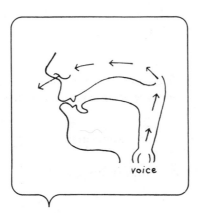

 Close your lips.
Use your voice.
m comes through your nose.

Practice 1 Listen and repeat:

Mm!	tomorrow	him	Smith
me	summer	Tim	small
met	family	time	smart
may	crumpets	come	Mum
make	Cambridge	some	home-made
maybe	remember	home	Tom Mitcham

Dialogue ## Mum's crumpets

Jim: *Mum, may Tom Mitcham come home with me for tea tomorrow?*

Mrs Smith: *Of course, Jim. Have I met Tom before?*

Jim: *You met him in the summer. He's very small and smart.*

Mrs Smith: *Oh, yes. I remember Tom. Does his family come from Cambridge?*

Jim: *Yes. Oh, Mum! Will you make some home-made crumpets tomorrow?*

Mrs Smith: *Mm . . . maybe. If I have time.*

Jim: *I told Tom about your crumpets, Mum. That's why he's coming for tea tomorrow!*

Intonation 'Mm' has many meanings.

 Practise these:

Mmm means 'What did you say?'

Mm means 'yes'.

Mmmmm means 'How nice!'

Now listen to this conversation and say which meaning 'Mm' has in B's answers.

A: Would you like some home-made crumpets?

B Mm?

A: Would you like some crumpets?

B: Mm.

A: Here you are.

B: (*eating*) Mm!

A: I'm glad you like them. I made them myself. Would you like to try them with marmalade?

B: Mm?
A: Marmalade. They're marvellous with marmalade. Would you like some?
B: Mm.
A: Here you are.
B: (*eating*) Mm!

Unit 44 n nose

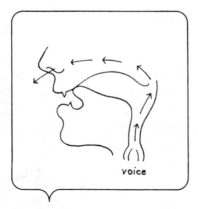

voice

Put your tongue on the roof of your mouth.
Touch your side teeth with the sides of your tongue.
Use your voice. n comes through your nose.

145

Practice 1 Listen and repeat:

	sound 1	sound 2	

me knee

$1.61\ km = 1\ m.$

mile Nile

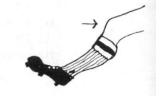

mine nine

Tim tin

comb cone

name mane

Test Tick the words you recognise in the sentences you hear:

1 a) combs; b) cones
2 a) mine; b) nine
3 a) name; b) mane
4 a) some; b) sun
5 a) warm; b) warn
6 a) money; b) mummy

Practice 2 Listen and repeat:

noise	apartment	Northend Avenue
morning	unfurnished	central London
rent	inexpensive	ninety-nine
agency	month	11.15
oven	station	garden
often	accommodation	kitchen
seven	television	Mr Mason
eleven	prison	certainly

Dialogue At an accommodation agency

Mr Mason : *Good morning. I want an apartment in central London.*
Manager : *Certainly, sir. How much rent did you want to pay?*
Mr Mason : *No more than £27 a month.*
Manager : *£27 a month? We don't often have apartments as inexpensive as that. We have one apartment for £29 a month in Northend Avenue. It's down near the station.*
Mr Mason : *Is it furnished?*
Manager : *No. It's unfurnished. The kitchen has no oven. It's forbidden to use the garden. No friends in the apartment after eleven in the evening. No noise and no television after 11.15. No . . .*
Mr Mason : *No thank you! I want an apartment, not a prison!*

Game Mini bingo

I	7	II	9	10	13	17	15	18	19
20	21	22	23	24	25	26	27	28	29
70	71	72	73	74	75	76	77	78	79
90	91	92	93	94	95	96	97	98	99

Play in a group of five people.
One person calls out the numbers above in any order.
The others each choose one of the boxes A, B, C or D below.
Cross out each number in your box as it is called (or put a
small piece of paper on top of each number as it is called).
The first person to cross out all his numbers wins.

A

9	20	99
15	79	71
97	19	10

B

I	79	II
13	9	7
99	27	10

C

77	79	99
18	19	97
II	91	29

D

I	79	9
17	19	18
99	21	70

Unit 45 ŋ ring

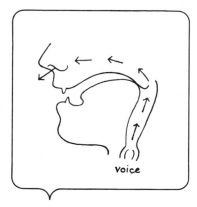

Voice

Touch the back of the roof of your mouth with the back of
your tongue.
Use your voice. ŋ comes through your nose.

Unit 45 ŋ (ring)

Practice 1 Listen and repeat:

sound 1 sound 2

win wing

thin thing

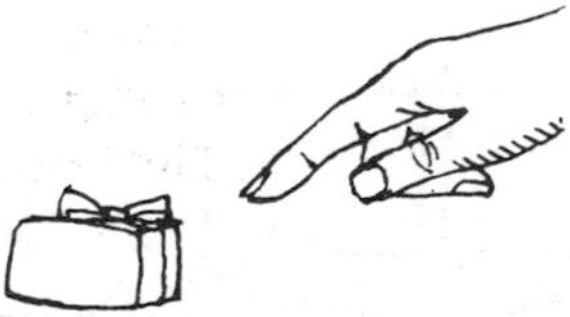

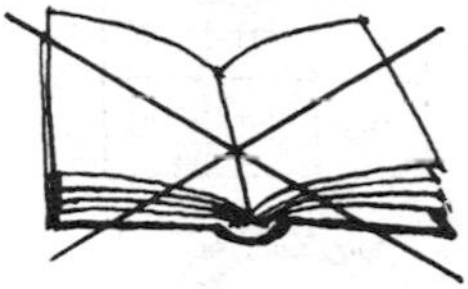

ban bang

ran rang

run rung

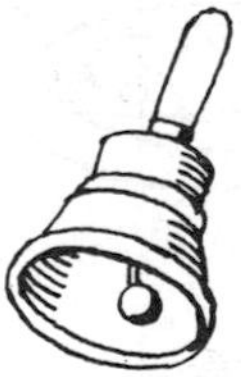

Ron wrong

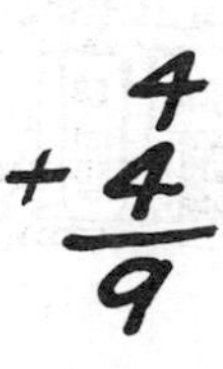

149

Practice 2   Listen and repeat:

| | sound 1 | sound 2 |

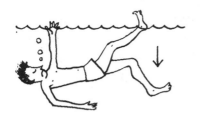

wink   wing

sink   sing

rink   ring

stink   sting

bank   bang

Unit 45   ŋ (ring)

Test   Tick the words you recognise in the sentences you hear:
1 a) Ron; b) wrong
2 a) ran; b) rang
3 a) sinks; b) sings
4 a) win; b) wink; c) wing
5 a) ban; b) bank; c) bang
6 a) sinners; b) sinkers; c) singers

Practice 3   Listen and repeat:

pink	Mr King	running
think	Mr Pring	ringing
drink	morning	singing
finger	something	bringing
angrily	standing	banging
	happening	hanging
	strong string	

Dialogue   Noisy neighbours

Mr Pring: (angrily). *Bang! Bang! Bang! What are the Kings doing at seven o'clock on Sunday morning?*

Mrs Pring: *Well, Mr King is singing.*

Mr Pring: *Yes, but what's the banging noise?*

Mrs Pring: (looking out of the window) *He's standing on a ladder and banging some nails into the wall with a hammer. Now he's hanging some strong string on the nails.*

Mr Pring: *And what's Mrs King doing?*

Mrs Pring: *She's bringing something pink for Mr King to drink. Now she's putting it under the ladder, and . . . Ohh!*

Mr Pring: *What's happening?*

Mrs Pring: *The ladder's falling.*

Mr Pring: *What's Mr King doing?*

Mrs Pring: *He's hanging from the string. He's holding the string in his fingers and he's shouting to Mrs King.*

Mr Pring: *And is she helping him?*

Mrs Pring: *No. She's running to our house. Now she's ringing our bell.*

Mr Pring: *I'm not going to answer it. I'm sleeping.*

151

Conversation   Talk about these pictures.

Example:

Mrs Pring

What's Mrs Pring doing?
She's looking out of the window.

1

Mr King

2

Mr King

3

Mrs King

4

Mr King

5.   6

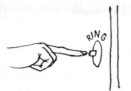 

Mrs King   Mr Pring

Unit 46 l letter Part 1

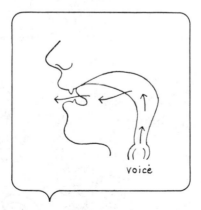

First practise n (see page 145).
To make l, the air goes over the sides of your tongue and out of your mouth.

Practice 1   Listen and repeat:

	sound 1	sound 2
	no	low

night   light

nine   line

Jenny   jelly

bin   Bill

ten   tell

154

Test Tick the words you recognise in the sentences you hear:

1 a) night; b) light
2 a) no; b) low
3 a) Jenny; b) jelly
4 a) knot; b) lot
5 a) snow; b) slow
6 a) snacks; b) slacks

Practice 2 Look at the picture. Then answer the questions.

Who's late for lunch?
What's Mr Lee looking at?
Is there a lot of lemonade left or only a little?
Is there any lettuce left?
Why is Mr Lee complaining?

Mr Allen

Who's lovely?
Who's early for lunch?
What's Mr Allen saying to Lily?
Is Mr Allen looking marvellous?
What's Mr Allen having for lunch?

Practice 3   Look at the picture. Then answer the questions.

What colour are the olives?
How many slices of melon does Mr Allen want?
Where are the black olives?
Where's the lemonade?

Dialogue   Early for lunch

Mr Allen: *Hello Lily. You're looking lovely today.*
Waitress: *Hello, Mr Allen. You're early for lunch. It's only eleven
           o'clock.*
Mr Allen: *When I come later there's usually nothing left.*
Waitress: *What would you like?*
Mr Allen: *Leg of lamb, please.*
Waitress: *And would you like a plate of salad?
           It's lettuce with black olives.*
Mr Allen: *Marvellous! I love olives.*
Waitress: *And would you like a glass of lemonade?*
Mr Allen: *Yes please, Lily. And a slice of melon and some yellow
           jelly.*

157

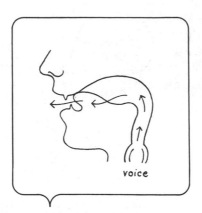

 In these words l has a slightly different sound:

Bill	help	uncle
Paul	myself	bicycle
tell	holding	careful
fall	difficult	beautiful
pull	salesman	sensible
I'll	a spoilt child	special
small	always	little
	fault	gentleman

Dialogue ## A spoilt little boy in a bicycle shop

Paul: *What a beautiful bicycle!*

Uncle Bill: *Paul! Be careful!*

Salesman: *Excuse me, sir. This child is too small to ride this bicycle. It's a very difficult bicycle to . . .*

Uncle Bill: *Be careful, Paul!*

Paul: *You always tell me to be careful. Don't help me. I won't fall.*

Salesman: *But, sir. This is a very special bicycle. It's . . .*

Paul: *Don't pull the bicycle, Uncle Bill. I'll do it myself.*

Uncle Bill: *Be sensible, Paul. This gentleman says it's a . . .*
(Paul falls)

Paul: *It was Uncle Bill's fault. He was holding the bicycle.*

Intonation Listen and repeat:
What a **tall** gentleman!
What a **won**derful apple!

Conversation Example: gentleman.
A: Look at that gentleman.
B: What a tall gentleman!

tall

1 needle   2 candle   3 apple

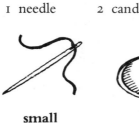      

small   **litt**le   **horr**ible

4 child   5 bottle   6 table

miserable   **beau**tiful   **won**derful

7 hospital   8 pencil   9 bicycle

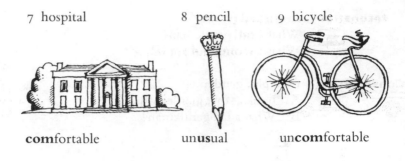

comfortable   un**us**ual   un**com**fortable

Unit 48   r   rain Part 1

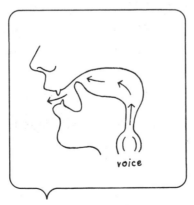

voice

🔲   Turn the tip of your tongue up as in the picture.
Do not touch the roof of your mouth with your tongue.
The sides of your tongue should touch your back teeth.

Practice 1   Listen and repeat:

	sound 1	sound 2
	long	wrong
	light	right
	load	road
	jelly	Jerry
	fly	fry
	glass	grass

$$+\dfrac{\begin{array}{r}4\\4\end{array}}{9}$$

$$+\dfrac{\begin{array}{r}4\\4\end{array}}{8}$$

Test

Tick the words you recognise in the sentences you hear:

1 a) long; b) wrong   4 a) collect; b) correct
2 a) jelly; b) Jerry   5 a) lane; b) rain
3 a) glass; b) grass   6 a) flea; b) free

Practice 2

Listen and repeat:

Ruth	very	pretty	grown up
Rita	Jerry	proud	Greece
Rosemary	Paris	France	drives
Mrs Reed	married	waitress	
restaurant	parent	countries	
Russia	America	Austria	
	everywhere in	interesting	
	Europe	secretary	

Practice 3

Listen and repeat:

railway	Laura	cleverest
really	lorry	electrician
Roland	library	children
Mrs Randal	librarian	Australia

Dialogue

A proud parent

Mrs Randal: *Are all the children grown up now, Ruth?*

Mrs Reed: *Oh, yes. Laura is the cleverest one. She's a librarian in the public library.*

Mrs Randal: *Very interesting. And what about Rita?*

Mrs Reed: *She's a secretary at the railway station.*

Mrs Randal: *And what about Rosemary? She was always a very pretty child.*

Mrs Reed: *Rosemary is a waitress in a restaurant in Paris. She's married to an electrician.*

Mrs Randal: *And what about Jerry and Roland?*

Mrs Reed: *Jerry drives a lorry. He drives everywhere in Europe.*

Mrs Randal: *Really? Which countries does he drive to?*

Mrs Reed: *France and Austria and Greece and Russia.*

Mrs Randal: *And does Roland drive a lorry too?*

Mrs Reed: *Oh, no. Roland is a pilot.*

Mrs Randal: *Really? Which countries does he fly to?*

Mrs Reed: *Australia and America.*

162

Conversation   Ask somebody these questions about Mrs Reed's children.

Example: Laura   train driver (librarian)
A: Is Laura a train driver?
B: No, she isn't. She's a librarian.

1 Jerry   electrician (lorry driver)
2 Rosemary   secretary (waitress)
3 Roland   photographer (pilot)
4 Rita   waitress (secretary)
5 Laura   lorry driver (librarian)

Unit 49   r   girl Part 2

New York	later	quarter
depart	weather	airport
afternoon	announcer	order
passengers	sir	earlier
forbidden	are	departure
wonderful	beer	forecaster
German	dear	supermarket
upstairs	four	Dr Darling
marvellous	more	Mr Martin
emergency	there	
storm	sure	
worse		

The letter 'r' is silent in these words.
When there is no vowel following it, 'r' is silent.

Dialogue   In this dialogue every letter 'r' is silent.

In the airport

Announcer:	*The 2.30 plane to New York will depart later this afternoon at four forty-four. Passengers on this flight are forbidden to leave the airport.*
Dr Darling:	*Wonderful! I'm going to the bar to order some more German beer.*
Mr Martin:	*Where's the bar?*
Dr Darling:	*It's upstairs. There's a bookshop too. And a supermarket. This is a marvellous airport!*
Mr Martin:	*Oh dear! I wanted to get to New York earlier. Ah! Here's an air hostess.*
	Excuse me. I don't understand. Has there been an emergency?
Air hostess:	*Oh, no, sir. There's just a storm, and the weather forecast says it will get worse. So the plane will leave a little later this afternoon.*
Mr Martin:	*Are you sure?*
Air hostess:	*Oh, yes, sir. Our departure time is at four forty-four.*

Tests

Unit 2
1 He wants a sheep for his birthday.
2 That's a very small bin.
3 Look at these chicks.
4 It's a cheap machine.
5 What a high heel!
6 Don't eat that pill.

Unit 3
1 You've dropped a pin.
2 That's a big peg.
3 Please give me tins.
4 Sit the baby on the table.
5 My friend's name is Jenny.
6 The bird pecked up the food.

Unit 4
1 I've bought a new pan.
2 Did you see the men?
3 He is sad to live alone.
4 That's a very expensive jam.
5 Don't pet the dog.
6 These are bed clothes.

Unit 5
1 What a dirty cap!
2 This hut is too small.
3 There's a black bug on the table.
4 They live in a mad house.
5 I hang my coat on the door.
6 The children run quickly.

Unit 6
1 He's broken my heart.
2 That's a very bad cut.
3 I gave him a cap.
4 There's a mouse in this barn.
5 Why don't you come down?
6 I don't like Patty's.

Unit 8
1 What a pretty little cot!
2 He tried to put his head in a sack.
3 The top was made of metal.
4 My friend's name is Tammy.
5 I liked the baddie in that film.
6 Write in block letters.

Unit 9
1 I don't like these sports.
2 These pots are very dirty.
3 Look at that white cord on the water.
4 Mr Smith was shot.
5 The lion walked towards Tom and Rod.
6 I said, 'What a dog!'

Unit 10
1 That cook is very noisy.
2 Lock it up carefully.
3 He's my godfather.
4 How do you spell 'cod'?
5 I call my cat Poss.
6 Her name is Miss Brookhurst.

Unit 11
1 Look, I want you to come here.
2 I said, 'He's full'.
3 The sign on the door said 'Pool'.
4 That's a foolish dress.

Unit 12
1 That a very small bed.
2 He's got a lot of buns.
3 That's a very long ward.
4 Why don't you walk faster?
5 She always wears shirt dresses.
6 His name's John ... er ... Thomas, I think.

Unit 13
1 He **has**n't finished his lunch.
2 C**ə**n you understand me?
3 Where w**ə**s Mary?
4 What d**ə**s he eat for lunch?
5 **Am** I late?
6 Put th**ə**m on the table.

Unit 15
1 This student has a very bad pen.
2 Let's sit in the shed.
3 Please give me some more pepper.
4 The children were late out from school.
5 Her letter writing is very good.
6 Open the door and get ready to leave.

Unit 16
1 I want a new cart.
2 The old lady was dining.
3 What a big star!
4 She has a good life.
5 This leather's hard.
6 Do you like pie?

Unit 17
1 Look at that gold coin.
2 The little boy was boiling with anger.
3 Look! It's all on the floor.
4 Aw! You've broken that glass.
5 He's a terrible boy.
6 Did you put all of it in the salad?

Unit 19
1 The bus drove into the car.
2 There's a lot of grass near the farm.
3 Her brow was white.
4 'Ha!' he said loudly.
5 'Ow!' he said, 'You hit me.'
6 Near the mountain there is a little town.

Unit 20
1 Have I put some cork in your glass?
2 They have a nice green fern in the hall.

3 You can have coffee. Or do you want tea?
4 Please don't throw that bowl.
5 Don't burn the chicken.
6 I walk early in the morning.

Unit 22
1 I've just swallowed a beer.
2 The tea fell on the floor.
3 What a funny bead!
4 What a lovely green pier!
5 There should be two 'e's and you've only got one.
6 How are you, dear?

Unit 23
1 'Three cheers', he said.
2 There was a small bear on the table.
3 That's a very big pier.
4 Look! It's here.
5 Can I borrow your pen, please, Dan, dear?
6 He said her name but it wasn't Claire.

Unit 25
1 That's a very small bin.
2 My friend's name is Poppy.
3 That pup is very noisy.
4 It's a pig house.
5 Put it on the horse's back.
6 What a lovely peach!

Unit 27
1 I don't like riding.
2 That's a nice cart.
3 He bought a bat, racquet and some balls.
4 I send all the parcels by air mail.
5 Do you like tarts?
6 I want to dry this shirt.

Unit 29
1 That man looks like a gold fish.
2 There's a fly on your back.

3 My grandmother bought a Dutch clock.
4 What a beautiful curl!
5 There a green frog in the garden.
6 The detective was looking for a good glue.

Unit 31
1 I heard a buzz.
2 Sip it slowly.
3 What's the price?
4 I only have a few pens.
5 'Help, please!' he shouted.
6 He lived in a town called Sackville.

Unit 32
1 I like Sue's.
2 Look at that dirty ash.
3 'Puss!' he shouted.
4 The mice lived in a shack.
5 I'm going to buy some new seats.
6 Tom should save.

Unit 34
1 That's a very expensive chop.
2 Would you like to drink cherry brandy or wine?
3 He's washing the television.
4 I like ships.
5 I fell down and cut my shin.
6 I want to choose, please.

Unit 35
1 I'm choking.
2 That's a large tree.
3 He bought a cheap type of car.
4 This is my new watch, Jane.
5 It's chilly in the garden.
6 The crowd jeered when he finished speaking.

Unit 36
1 That's a long fin.
2 Peel this orange.
3 She walked round the garden sniffing flowers.

4 Please feel this shoe.
5 Mr Pearson is a hat seller.
6 That's a very big hole.

Unit 37
1 This room has a few.
2 Halve the apple.
3 New York is a fast city.
4 We've got the boat.
5 There should be fifty bolts.
6 I don't like the sound of his fowls.

Unit 38
1 What a beautiful vine!
2 He wrote 'we' at the beginning of the sentence.
3 Please change this veal.
4 This book is worse.
5 We were surprised to see some whales in the water.
6 Look! That viper's gone from the car now.

Unit 39
1 That's a bad yolk.
2 Let's eat jam.
3 Jess, let's go to the cinema.
4 These were terrible years for him.
5 What juice is that?
6 He hasn't flown by jet.

Unit 40
1 I don't like these eels.
2 He hurt his foot and leg and arm.
3 These children have got beautiful high brows.
4 Do you like heart?
5 'How!' he shouted loudly.
6 What lovely air!

Unit 41
1 I always sink in the bath.
2 What a small mouth!
3 Don't burn it. That saucepan is only tin.

4 The teacher thought quickly.

5 Look at that moss on that stone.

6 The two men fought very hard.

Unit 42

1 I don't like her sister, Ida.

2 Day came suddenly.

3 Jim dares his friend.

4 That's a very large size.

5 Did you sea bathe?

6 The booth echoed loudly.

Unit 44

1 I want two cones, please.

2 I'll give you nine.

3 What a beautiful mane!

4 I only want sun flowers.

5 Please warm the children.

6 He loves his mummy.

Unit 45

1 That's Ron.

2 Somebody rang.

3 Tom always sinks in the bath.

4 What a beautiful wink!

5 You should bang it.

6 This is not the right place for sinkers.

Unit 46

1 Look! The moon's shining. What a lovely night!

2 There are no tables here.

3 Tom loves Jenny.

4 It's a lot of string.

5 I'm wearing snow shoes.

6 I'm going to buy some slacks.

Unit 48

1 That sentence is long.

2 Susan likes Jerry.

3 There's some glass in the garden.

4 Please collect the homework.

5 We walked in the rain.

6 This is a free house.

Review units: answers to recorded tests

Unit 7

1. (bud) sound 5
2. (ban) sound 4
3. (ɪ) sound 2
4. (peak) sound 1
5. (e) sound 3
6. (bard) sound 6
7. (bad) sound 4
8. (peck) sound 3
9. (iː) sound 1
10. (bean) sound 1

Unit 14

1. (ɜː) sound 5
2. (fool) sound 4
3. (wooed) sound 4
4. (ʊ) sound 3
5. (ward) sound 2
6. (word) sound 5
7. (ɒ) sound 1
8. (could) sound 3
9. (curd) sound 5
10. (what) sound 1

Unit 18

1. (ɔɪ) sound 3
2. (isle) sound 2
3. (ale) sound 1
4. (eɪ) sound 1
5. (Royce) sound 3
6. (race) sound 1
7. (point) sound 3
8. (bay) sound 1
9. (rice) sound 2
10. (oil) sound 3

Unit 21

1. (əʊ) sound 2
2. (found) sound 1
3. (load) sound 2
4. (loud) sound 1
5. (aʊ) sound 1
6. (no) sound 2

MASK
Cut along
the dotted
line